Soil Science

A Step-by-step Action Plan to Quickly Grow Soil

(Immerse Yourself in Transformation Techniques That Promise a Prosperous)

Hector Redford

Published By **Oliver Leish**

Hector Redford

All Rights Reserved

Soil Science: A Step-by-step Action Plan to Quickly Grow Soil (Immerse Yourself in Transformation Techniques That Promise a Prosperous)

ISBN 978-1-988842-03-5

No part of this guidebook shall be reproduced in any form without permission in writing from the publisher except in the case of brief quotations embodied in critical articles or reviews.

Legal & Disclaimer

The information contained in this book is not designed to replace or take the place of any form of medicine or professional medical advice. The information in this book has been provided for educational & entertainment purposes only.

The information contained in this book has been compiled from sources deemed reliable, and it is accurate to the best of the Author's knowledge; however, the Author cannot guarantee its accuracy and validity and cannot be held liable for any errors or omissions. Changes are periodically made to this book. You must consult your doctor or get professional medical advice before using any of the suggested remedies, techniques, or information in this book.

Upon using the information contained in this book, you agree to hold harmless the Author from and against any damages, costs, and expenses, including any legal fees potentially resulting from the application of any of the information provided by this guide. This disclaimer applies to any damages or injury caused by the use and application, whether directly or indirectly, of any advice or information presented, whether for breach of contract, tort, negligence, personal injury, criminal intent, or under any other cause of action.

You agree to accept all risks of using the information presented inside this book. You need to consult a professional medical practitioner in order to ensure you are both able and healthy enough to participate in this program.

Table Of Contents

Chapter 1: Soil Basics Knowing Your Soil

Not an entire lot grows out of doors while its miles cold, wet, and cloudy from late October till spring. Even plant life grown under a cloche or in a greenhouse will expand slowly due to the reality they should art work difficult to reveal the low light into power for photosynthetic interest. Now is the excellent time of 365 days to have a have a look at soil technological know-how and think about a manner to improve your garden soil before you plant new seeds or transplants in the spring. You can learn greater approximately lawn soil and the way it is able to be modified by way of searching at 4 essential topics. These are the soil's texture, make-up, life, and pH. Gardeners will do higher within the event that they reflect onconsideration on the ones four things separately and collectively.

How the soil is made and the way it feels

This is about what number of portions of dust there are. Clay, silt, and sand are three of them. The soil's houses, like its capacity to maintain water, get difficult and permit water through, relying on how large those tiny particles are.

Sand: Even if the quantities are as thin as salt and sugar on a table, the granules are despite the fact that quite big. Sand is manufactured from small rocks that have been beaten. Different silicate compounds may be used to make it. Sand is made of huge portions which might be separated with the aid of massive areas. This shall we water dry out speedy. Sand grains are big, virtually so that they do not waft spherical inside the soil a whole lot.

Silt: Silt debris are an lousy lot smaller than sand and are made with the useful resource of physical breaking them up. If you need to evaluate it to sand, keep in mind finely ground flour in preference to coarse salt. Silt is crafted from very small portions, making it smooth to transport via the soil. It makes a massive difference in how properly the soil can stick collectively.

Clay: Close together, these quantities look like plates. In assessment to silt and sand, clay is made while acids within the soil and water spoil down elements. Clay soils can be 1,000 instances smaller than sand grains, which makes herbal clay revel in unique and smooth. Because clay sticks collectively so nicely, its pores and outflow can be very small.

When they communicate approximately soil shape, professionals communicate about everything from pleasant sand to clay. The high-quality shape of soil shape is "loam." 40% is silt, 40% is sand, and 20% is clay. It is right at shielding water and making lumps. When it dries, it does not get hard and stick together. Instead, it's far clean to break apart. Since the granules in particular loam are all special sizes, the areas amongst them also are terrific, which is good for permeability.

Soil Life

How properly organic gardening works is based totally upon on how a whole lot "existence" is in the soil. One professional who wrote a e-book on the assignment says that "microorganisms need to be overflowing" in a wholesome surroundings. There are also many odd animals residing in the soil. Think about what number of splendid sorts of soil organisms there are normal with acre of accurate soil in kilos:

Even despite the fact that you probably do now not recollect what 900 kilos of earthworms appear to be, they and specific dwelling matters are vital for the soil to paintings. Microbes in the soil change the minerals in herbal compounds into compounds that plants can use. Many, like micro organism, can do many numerous matters and assist the soil restore nitrogen from the air. Some animals, like earthworms, make the soil greater healthful with the resource of turning it, similar to what we do with a fork. When they arrive to the ground to devour, they pull all the nutrients deeper into the soil, wherein the roots can achieve them or wherein one in every of a kind sorts of micro organism at amazing depths can exchange them in unique methods. In herbal gardening, you upload natural remember to the soil, feeding flora and animals. Plants increase more sincerely while the soil includes amazing styles of wholesome organisms. So that we are able to eat plant life, we ought to take vitamins from the soil and positioned them into the plant life. Organic farmers constantly attempt to beautify the soil via the use of including greater natural rely variety.

Soil pH

Another element that impacts soil fitness has much less to do with its biological and chemical homes. "Potential hydrogen" is what the letter pH stands for. As the water drops land on the ground or is watered into the soil, they come to be a part of a chemical aggregate. The pH scale measures the stableness among the incredible and terrible hydroxide ions.

Some water particles mixture with minerals within the soil to make new compounds, while others mix with clay and compost to make acids. These chemical methods change the top soil's alkalinity or acidity with out going into too much element. Soil this is neither too acidic nor too alkaline is wanted via almost all flowers that people eat.

The pH scale commonly runs from 1 (very acidic, like stomach acid) to 14. (very alkaline, much like lye). Purified water has a pH of seven.Zero, that is idea to be the maximum balanced stage.

A home gardener can take a look at the pH of the soil in distinct techniques.

If the topsoil is simply too acidic or alkaline, it is extra hard for plants to get the vitamins they want to growth. These topics furthermore make it easier for other things which may be horrible for the soil to get in. Wet, acidic soil moreover upsets the stableness of existence within the soil because it enables a few microbial cells develop at the same time as preventing others. Because of this, gardeners should continuously take steps to alternate the pH of the topsoil in their location.

Soil Composition

Every gardener must be aware of mineral rely, soil air, herbal depend amount, and soil water. Here's what the ones four additives appear like at their maximum number one stage. Mineral content - 45% Soil air - 25% Soil water - 25% Organic cloth - five% There are many one-of-a-kind types of microorganisms within the soil, together with rodents, insects, nematodes, bacteria, fungus, and algae. Organic and mineral depend make up the vast part of a three-section device, which moreover has answers of water, salts, and powerful gases. Different gases make up the gaseous segment. Each step of the tool has many terrific components, making it difficult to understand. Because the soil adjustments, its atmosphere is never in balance.

Chapter 2: Preparing Your Soil For Planting

Putting seeds within the floor isn't always the way you start a garden. Everything begins offevolved with the soil. Without rich, smooth topsoil that we could the roots develop deep sufficient to gain vitamins, it is impossible to increase healthful, powerful flora. The nicely data is that compost and wonderful herbal substances can help your soil get higher. Organic be counted variety is broken down with the useful resource of earthworms and different tiny creatures into minerals that flora want. This offers the soil life of its personal.

It drains well, breaks up the soil so flowers can get extra oxygen, keeps nutrients and water, and continues soil biota stable and related.

We do not need to be so tough on a gardener genuinely starting that they surrender! Here are the three maximum important steps for spring, but we are able to talk greater approximately preparing the soil beneath.

Take the garbage and rocks away. After decreasing the sod into small portions, pull the grasses out of the plantation area with the stop of the shovel.

Break up the ground. If this is your first time gardening, cut up the soil to a depth of at the least eight inches, but 12 inches is higher, so the roots can boom deep...

Tell me approximately the natural depend: Even if all you may do inside the spring is add herbal materials like compost, you'll be off to an first-rate start. When the soil is damp however not soaked, that is the day to add. On pinnacle of your topsoil, placed 2 to a few inches of well-elderly herbal manure (and not above 4 ins). Several gardeners will positioned the flowers and flora at the ground.

Leaving the compost on pinnacle is some other manner to do it. This will maintain the feel of the soil and make it harder for weeds to develop. Let the worms do the tough paintings of digging. Experts say that how your Earth is made makes a large distinction. Use manure if the topsoil is already lousy after the primary three hundred and sixty five days. But in case your soil is hard and compact, you can need to construct a raised mattress. You also can extend in bins like pots. Before you plant, use a metal lawn rake to diploma the raised beds.

Here are a few ideas that might assist you put together the soil:

How to get your topsoil warmness: If you live in a cooler region, you'll in all likelihood want to apply an accelerated lawn mattress to help the moist, bloodless soil dry out and warmth up quicker. Before you plant, you may furthermore cowl your beds with black fabric or newspaper to dam the solar and guard them from rain, frost, and runoff.

The proper manner to put off weeds: You can cast off weeds earlier than it's time to plant by means of way of lightly turning the top layer of soil and warming it with sheets of clean plastic. Again, whilst the weed seedlings have grown, you can pull them out through hand or with a hoe. The goal is to cast off the already seen weeds. More weeds will come to the ground if you dig into the soil.

Once you have got a base of deep, healthy, black soil, gardening can be smooth for the rest of the year and for future years.

Chapter 3: How To Perform Soil Tests

The soil wishes to be wholesome for gardening to art work. Most of the time, it influences how plant life develop or die greater than light and water. The splendid manner to find out how appropriate your topsoil is and its pH degree is to check it.

Why a soil check is crucial

Crops ought to be able to get what they need from the soil. Your vegetation can't live properly with out those nutrients. If the pH of your soil is proper, flora can get the vitamins they want from it (degree of acid content material). If your acidity is actually too immoderate, it'll in all likelihood be difficult to get to minerals like phosphate and iron. If your hobby is sincerely too low, plant life may moreover emerge as poisonous. It's tough to have an first rate lawn without right soil.

We take a look at the soil, so we do no longer must add too much fertilizer, some other detail. The soil might not need "repair" if it's far healthful. You ought to take a sample of the soil and deliver it to a lab for sorting out earlier than you may start including calcium and fertilizers.

The results of the soil take a look at

A proper soil test can assist you to apprehend if your soil is frequently sand, silt, or clay and the way acidic it is with the aid of using measuring its pH diploma. There can be a calculation of methods lots carbonate, magnesium, calcium, and potassium are to be had. Suggestions may be made for developing each mineral to the right degree for the awesome plant boom.

Now which you recognize this, you could make the crucial changes. Use the soil test effects as a manual because of the fact an excessive amount of of a great component can be just as horrible as now not sufficient.

How to check your soil

Check your soil's pH and mineral content material cloth each 3 to five years for the pleasant plant growth. Soil samples can be taken at any time of the one year. You need to nonetheless fall. This is a tremendous way to find out the way you probable did and what you want to change earlier than summer season.

Places to check the soil

You can purchase checking out kits at lawn facilities, however they will be not as correct or thorough as tests carried out thru a county extension agent on your vicinity. The cool trouble is that most close by extension offices offer reasonably-priced or loose soil tests. The National Institute of

Food and Agriculture has listed community extension offerings that you may look at.

How to Pick a Random Soil Sample for a Test

Clear the ground of any dust, plant additives, twigs, and so forth., to get a random pattern.

Never take a test in a place in which a person has burned brush, piled manure or compost, or positioned down ashes.

Dig a V-formed trench in the floor six to 8 inches deep with a spade or trowel.

Cut a 1-inch-huge piece of Earth and a small piece of the hollow.

Cut a one-inch strip from the center of this slice to make your pattern.

Do this all over the region, and then positioned the results in a field or bucket product of easy glass.

Because we use raised beds, you're taking a piece from each area and mix them.

You want to diploma out a cup of dust, allow it dry for a few days, and then placed it in a Ziploc bag together along with your call and make contact with amount.

Send it in with the required paperwork and price, and then look ahead to the effects!

DIY Soil Testing

Here are 3 simple tests you could do yourself to decide if your soil is rough or clean.

The peanut butter jar test to discover how the soil feels

Find out what your soil is like! The exceptional soil has 20% clay, 40% silt, and 40% sand. This want to take approximately an hour to installation and all day to complete. Find a jar with a lid and at once elements, like a mason jar or a jar of peanut butter, and preserve a ruler available. Start digging in the area you want to take a look at till you gain the roots, approximately 6 inches down. Take out sufficient dirt to fill about half of of of the jar. Then, positioned water within the neck of the jar and permit it sit down for some time so the soil can soak it up. Once the lid is on, shake the jar hard for three mins.

After you located down the container, check your watch. Use the ruler to decide how an entire lot stuff is at the lowest after one minute. This is what the sand seems like within the topsoil.

Wait 4 mins extra. Again, observe the sand: The distinction between the 2 numbers

will show how lots silt is in your soil.

Do the 1/3 analyzing the following day. The difference a number of the second and 1/three numbers suggests how masses clay is for your soil.

Find out how tons clay, silt, and sand you will need. The sum want to add as masses as a hundred%. There ought to be 20% clay, forty% silt, and forty% sand in correct topsoil. Use this clean take a look at that will help you decide what to increase: Your soil will drain nicely if it has plenty of sand. It's tough to get silt or clay moist, however it remains that way as soon as it's miles. This is right for flowers that want to have "moist toes." Choose the proper plant life or exchange the soil:

Add nitrogen-rich compost, vintage manure, vermiculite, or sawdust in case your soil is sandy. The soil also can be stepped forward by which consist of thick, clay-wealthy soil.

Mix new straw with compost, nicely-rotted cow manure, pebbles, or coarse aggregate if your soil is sandy (not seaside sand).

Add high-quality sand (no longer seashore sand), compost, and peat moss to muddy soil.

The take a look at to discover the pH of the soil in the pantry

Fill a basin with 12 cups of vinegar and a pair of teaspoons of soil. The soil on top is alkaline if the solution bubbles up.

Put teaspoons of soil in a dish and cover it with filtered water. Include half cup bicarbonate of soda. The soil is acidic if the aggregate does not paintings.

If neither test works, the topsoil's pH is first-rate.

Plants can get ill or no longer get sufficient nutrients if the pH of the soil is just too excessive or too low. The pH scale goes from five.Five to 7, it is a balanced range. In this range, the most biodegradation takes location, and the maximum vitamins get to the roots of plant life. You can alternate the pH of your soil as quickly as what it's miles. Mixing finely overwhelmed lime into acidic (sour) soil can restore it on the same time as mixing floor sulfur into alkaline (candy) soil can restore it.

Chapter 4: How To Enrich Your Garden With Composting

Compost, crafted from herbal rely quantity, can be brought to the soil to help vegetation develop. More than 30% of our trash consists of food scraps and outside waste that might be composted. By making compost, the ones items do no longer turn out to be in landfills, in which they take in location and release methane and exclusive sturdy greenhouse gases. You want three subjects to make compost.

These embody

Brown substances: This consists of broken branches, leaves, and small twigs.

Green materials: Things like grass clippings, leftover veggies, fruit pits, and espresso ashes belong to this organisation.

Water: the right amount of easy water.

You should have an identical form of brown and inexperienced topics for your compost pile. Layers of herbal factors with debris of numerous sizes have to be modified. Your compost receives carbon from the brown factors, nitrogen from the green components, and moisture from the water, which facilitates the herbal keep in mind damage down.

You can use many stuff to make compost.

Fruits and veggies

Coffee grounds and filters

Eggshells

Bagged tea

Walnut shells

Crushed newspapers

Yard clippings and paper

Shreds of grass

Indoor vegetation

Straw and hay

Foliage

Sawdust

Chipped wooden

Wool and Cotton Scraps

Fireplace embers

Hairs and furs

You ought to no longer placed these items in your compost:

The branches or twigs of a black walnut tree: These factors will launch chemical compounds that might damage other flora.

Ash from charcoal or coals: This has chemical compounds that flowers do not like.

Rats and flies are interested by the smells of eggs and dairy products like margarine, milk, sour cream, and yogurt.

Plants with pests or illnesses: Pests or illnesses can stay spherical and spread to greater plants.

Fat, bacon, or oils— These subjects scent terrible, and bugs and rodents are interested in them.

Shells and scraps of fish or meat can odor horrible and attract flies and rats.

Dirty cat litter or poop from a canine or cat can also need to have bacteria, viruses, parasites, and unique topics which can make people ill.

Chemical pesticides on grass clippings have to kill organisms that help the composting tool.

Talk in your community's composting or waste manager to find out if the ones herbal materials may be picked up or dropped off with the useful aid of the composting service for your location.

Why composting is vital

It feeds the soil, which enables preserve water in it and stops pests and crop sicknesses.

It cuts down on how hundreds chemical fertilizers are needed.

It allows correct micro organism and fungi enlarge, which destroy down useless vegetation and animals to make humus, it's complete of vitamins.

It cuts down on how plenty carbon you produce and what type of greenhouse fuel your landfill offers off.

Tips for Home Composting

A compost pile may be made in masses of certainly one of a kind strategies. Here are a number of the fundamentals of the manner to do it. A pitchfork, a shovel, a machete with a squared-off blade, and a water hose with a twig head are useful equipment. Adding a bit water and turning or blending the compost on occasion will keep it in brilliant form.

Garden Composting

Put your compost pile or bin in a dry, shady area close to a water supply.

Add the brown and green portions as you get them, ensuring to cut or shred any quantities which is probably too big.

Add water as you add dry gadgets.

Chapter 5: Choosing The Right Irrigation Systems

Some vegetation need to be watered regularly, or even flora that could live in dry situations want a drink now after which. There are a whole lot of different factors which have an impact on the superb manner to water your flower beds.

These encompass:

Basic Water Needs

Vegetable gardens, grass, perennial plant life, and vegetation that could live in dry situations all want wonderful amounts of water. Consider how a whole lot water every plant will want while making plans your out of doors or garden. Group flowers that need the identical quantity of water collectively. When all of the plant life in a certain area get the identical amount of water simultaneously, it will probable be less hard to control irrigation (and could help conserve water)—maintaining the fitness of nearby plant life in take a look at through not overwatering plants that need a outstanding deal much less water or underwatering flowers that need extra water really because of the truth they'll be close to collectively. Also, maintain in mind that annuals with skinny roots need watering more frequently than perennials with deep roots.

Climate

For example, even as it's far heat and stormy or cold and foggy, extraordinary quantities of water and one in each of a type strategies to apply it are wanted. One of the outstanding subjects you may do in your garden is to pick out plants which can be proper for the Earth. For instance, you and your plant life will every be compelled in case you attempt to increase tropical flora in a barren place.

Rainfall

Changes can be made to rain every week, month, yr, or year. If you live in which Mother Nature seems after a number of the watering for you, make sure you've got a sprinkler device that you could alternate.

Type of Soil Surface

If you need water to go with the flow down a slope or live on a flat ground, you can need to follow it in a fine way and at a certain fee. Even on flat land, it may be hard to decide out how frequently and what sort of to water due to the truth water desires, soil sorts, and exposure all variety. Adding a hill to the aggregate makes it greater tough to water. Gravity, the slope of the route, and modifications in stress because of changes in altitude all want to be taken into consideration. Monitoring valves should additionally be put in at lower ranges so that any water though there could not leak out.

Sunlight

The robust sun can dry up to 50% of the water in a outside that gets quite some suns. Rainwater remains longer in dark locations, that could motive flooding. Find the one of a type additives or zones of your lawn as an entire. Drip or soaker irrigation is a brilliant manner to water flowers in areas with a whole lot of sun and wind because it continues water from evaporating. Zones continuously inside the color need to be watered at a particular time than those constantly inside the solar. This is because of the truth they may get an excessive amount of water faster than in warmer and drier places.

Soil Composition

How well a place can absorb and drain rainwater is based upon at the way it seems, whether or not sandy, clayey, wealthy, or mountainous. Clay soil is frequently defined by using manner of using the phrase "heavy."

Clay can maintain masses of water, which spreads out and soaks in slowly. Clay soil needs to be watered slowly to soak up the water. Clay soil is tough for roots to get into, and as it dries out, it has a dishonest to interrupt aside.

When compost or one-of-a-kind living subjects are introduced to clay soil, it absorbs water better. Rainwater won't live in sandy soil for lengthy, so it seeps right via. Plants want to be watered extra often and over a larger area to develop roots. Adding compost or one-of-a-kind natural materials is the pleasant way to maintain water within the soil. The high-quality soil for developing flora is loam, sand, silt, and clay. Loam is full of vitamins, distributes water well, and we could water drain nicely.

Common Irrigation Techniques

How you solution the questions above will determine the top notch manner to water your flowers. Here are a number of the maximum famous options:

Mini Sprinklers

Water-spraying Pop-up underground structures are most customarily used to water lawns or spread water over a sizable place. Depending on the dimensions and shape of your grass, you can trade how and in which its waters. They also are generally a good deal inexpensive than awesome choices.

Drip Watering System

You can find exactly wherein the water goes (emitters) with tubes and nozzles. Putting in drip irrigation systems takes some planning, but they store water through putting it high-quality in which it is wanted and slowly enough that it does now not run off or get too heat.

Portable Sprinklers

These are probably the least steeply-priced manner to shop for the tool, however they're now not normally the super. They are, but, pinnacle for placing water in a small place.

Watering Can

A smooth watering can paintings in case you handiest have some flower pots or a very small lawn. You can also use them to water plants interior.

Automatic Irrigation

If you've got timers, controls, and valves that could activate and rancid the water go with the flow primarily based on a time table or the weather, you may sincerely automate watering your backyard.

Most estimates of crop manufacturing and intake are based totally on how crops did in the beyond. You can parent out your vegetable lawn goals and plan higher through manner of retaining a food diary and garden document. How the garden is set up and what varieties of plants are planted will determine how many veggies can be grown. The yield would possibly trade from season to season, counting on the weather and the plant's boom.

You can parent out how huge your house vegetable garden should be through manner of way of identifying what number of greens you may grow and how many different types you need to grow for every member of the family.

We've included crop production estimates, plant-steady with-individual guidelines, and crop percentage requirements that will help you determine how big your flora receives and what kind of place you can want to your lawn. Use those estimates alongside facet what .

Choosing Where to Grow: Raised Beds,

Ground, or Containers

Once the manner masses you need to plant, you want to determine in which you may plant it. There are nearly too many kinds of gardens to rely, but they may be positioned into 3 groups: raised beds, in-floor gardens, and gardens in packing containers. After we speak in brief approximately the professionals and cons of every, you may determine which one (or a mixture of them) is awesome for you and your location.

Raised Beds

When most human beings consider a vegetable lawn, they photo flora growing on raised beds. Raised beds are each square or square systems with soil indoors to increase flowers. There may be a difference of their pinnacle and duration. I may not say I don't like raised beds due to the fact I now use them in my garden. We love ours, however it is apparent that everything has execs and cons.

Pros

1.   You are in full manipulate: When I plant in raised beds, I can maintain an eye fixed on everything, it is the super issue. I'm responsible for the weeds, insects, dirt, vegetation, watering, and plant life.

2.   Deep planting: The roots of plants flow down an extended way. They want wealthy, crumbly soil to dig in. Because they will be better off the floor, raised beds

deliver the roots extra room to develop, even extra so if you make tall raised beds.

three. Safe and clean: If the beds are better, you do now not need to bend over masses, this is higher for your once more. You need to drag out fewer weeds due to the reality you have got got extra manipulate over the surroundings.

four. No-until: After you fill your beds with appropriate soil, you can no longer should worry about digging or the use of heavy machines.

Cons:

1. Costly: You need topics to make raised beds. People regularly construct raised beds out of vintage pallets for little or no price, however we provided substances for every bed for approximately $one hundred fifty and choice they may remaining for many years.

2.   It takes time to collect and fill: Putting together and filling raised beds, specially large ones, can take a long term. But once it's performed, it's miles completed for genuine; it's miles a one-time problem.

three. Excess watering: Since raised beds aren't within the ground, they will short lose water. Because of this, you may have to water raised beds extra regularly.

four. Growth in a small area: When you upload raised beds and paths, the gap you have got were given for flora to growth is routinely lessen down. Still, some topics may be achieved. The Square Foot Gardening technique is first rate for humans who've in no manner gardened earlier than and those who do not have plenty room.

In-Ground

The time-examined way. Cut the grass, put together the ground, plant seeds, and watch them increase! It is that clean. Actually, now not quite. Growing plants inside the floor is a tougher way to do it, but if you do it proper, it may be cheap and productive. Let's talk approximately what's suitable and horrific approximately it.

Pros:

1.   Inexpensive: The fee of this mission have become saved low because of the truth the best device wanted were a shovel and a spade (rentable).

2.   Ease to begin: This sort of lawn might be organized to grow food in as low as a few hours.

3.   No limits on period or form: You ought to make a mattress in any length or form which you might imagine of. The plant life in our recovery garden are in the form of a triangle.

four.   Large yield: Most farmers who are suitable at what they do have a motive for planting inside the floor. Direct planting in the ground soil is the first-class way to increase the most veggies in your region.

5.	Less irrigation: Your plant will want a whole lot a lot much less watering than if you used raised beds or containers. This is due to the truth its roots are within the ground and might use all the rainwater seeping thru.

Cons

1.	Poor ground exceptional: Most people do now not have notable topsoil. A lot of adjustments will want to be made to the soil in advance than it may develop pinnacle greens. This is achieved thru setting matters all over again into the soil, like vermicompost, powders, and other organic materials.

2.	Weeds: Even after the sod has been pulled up, grass and extraordinary weeds keep growing. Weeds are so difficult that they'll develop once a soil spot is left empty.

three. Can seem unsightly: Even although some in-ground gardens are very pretty, they may be difficult to make because of how they may be made. If your landscape seems critical to you, you need to think about this.

four. Arduous exertions: Physical exertions can be preferred for the initial artwork (like digging out the topsoil and tilling) and ongoing protection (growing, plucking, and mulching).

Containers

Plant in bins if you have a small outside or live in an rental where you can't set up a lawn. You'll be surprised at how a amazing deal you could increase in only some pots in case you located them within the right places. Here are some of the specialists and cons:

Pros

1.   Occupy minimum room: You have to positioned a pot of greens on your patio, in all likelihood on a colorful shelf.

2.   Not lengthy-term: People who rent their homes or live in places in which it might be a crime to put a eternal garden can use containers to develop their flora.

3.   Little devotion: Don't understand whether or now not you need to lawn? With bins, it's far clean to test some thing out earlier than shopping for it. If you and your own family like to boom flora in a few pots, you would possibly get extra the following yr. But you may not lose some thing if you do not find it irresistible.

4.   Reasonably priced: You best need some big pots and luggage of herbal potting soil to begin. A clean vegetable garden can be commenced in a pot for much less than $50.

Cons:

1.   Affects growth: There isn't plenty room for planting in a pot, and there is not a great deal soil. This may want to make the roots get tangled or prevent the plant from getting the minerals it desires to amplify.

2.   Watering: Containers dry out quicker than the floor or raised beds, this is regularly vital.

three. Weight: Plant pots can be difficult to transport whilst they are complete of soil and flowers. So, ensure they are in that you need them to be.

Chapter 6: No-Until Gardening

When you figure hard, you get something lower again. But is digging that critical? Have you ever puzzled why turning the soil over every 12 months is essential? Mother Earth does not dig with a shovel, in the long run. So it should now not be a surprise that "no-dig" or "no-till" gardening is becoming an increasing number of famous with gardeners international.

Why it's miles no longer an terrific idea to dig earlier than you plant

Undoubtedly, digging is hard artwork, but maximum humans agree it's well worth it. It is supposed to soften and fluff up the soil, making it plenty much less complex to plant seeds and transplants. It want to moreover make it less difficult to mix in compost and other herbal materials that upload vitamins.

But, does it? Think about all the bacteria, earthworms, floor beetles, and fungi that get damage every time we dig.

Ripping on the soil slows down the normal steps that result in proper soil as it disrupts this complicated web of lifestyles. When the soil is not moved spherical, the topics that live in it could maintain growing.

This additionally enables soil bugs and the matters they consume get alongside better. When you dig loads, mainly at the same time as you double-dig, that is while you dig down with shovel blades, you get tired quick. It's also horrible for your lower lower back. Why then do it?

How to Start New Gardens without Tilling

Even despite the fact that there can be extra growth zones, there may be no want to dig. Try casting off the trash or rocks huge than a bird's egg. Trim wooden or grass to the floor. Add a thick layer of natural rely that has simply damaged down. This will stop the weeds from growing through blocking off the slight and deliver the roots a exquisite location to grow. At least 10 cm deep is wanted (four inches). You can use compost or manure from a reliable supply in that you recognize no insecticides were used.

After a few weeks, the worms may also want to have moved all of the herbal rely quantity wide variety into the soil, killing any grass or weeds below.

If there are some of weeds in the location wherein you want to grow flora, placed down a piece of cardboard earlier than you spread your natural compounds. To assist the card damage down, wet it all the way thru. Weeds will find out it greater difficult to grow thru the cardboard, killing most of them in the long run. Once the growing season begins offevolved, it's far going to be a good buy less difficult to do away with any weeds that try to live.

Use heavy, well-included cardboard to mark the paths a number of the beds. This will do away with the weeds which is probably growing between the constructing net internet web sites. At some factor, the card may be covered with wood chips or something else.

When it's time to plant, if the plant carbon in your soil remains bumpy, you have to begin vegetable seeds in plug pans or boxes. You can plant them outside as quickly as their roots are robust. Also, it will probably be smooth to area the vegetation calmly, saving time whilst you want to skinny out rows of seedlings.

How to Give Things a Natural Look

Using close by substances is a commonplace manner to construct and deal with the soil. Materials like woodchips are used to mimic how nature recycles nutrients again and again. Let's look at this method to make a bed. Start thru manner of overlaying the cleared ground with a thick layer of paper or cardboard. After the compost, add a layer of timber pellets approximately inches (5 cm) deep. Make first rate the 2 layers do now not get combined up. The woodchips can then be without trouble moved out of the way so that you can plant them within the compost underneath. You can also use some thing else, like hay or leaf mold, rather than woodchips. This top layer maintains water from evaporating and feeds the soil underneath simply so no more fertilizers is probably desired within the future.

Include Mulch

Adding layers of natural take into account is the crucial component to a garden that does not need to be tilled. Mulches prevent the soil's cowl from washing away, keep the soil moist, and save you weeds from developing. They decorate the soil's shape and fertility with out digging as they destroy down. In no-until gardening, the soil isn't dug up. You located down mulch as an opportunity.

Replace antique mulch as it breaks down or gets mixed into the soil to maintain feeding it and enhancing it. You can placed mulch spherical older flowers or wait till the developing season is over. Mulches may be product of leaf fungus, straw, woodchips, grass clippings, hay, and sawdust. Mulches can not paintings within the event that they've weed seeds in them, both.

Farming without tilling

No-till planting can art work for any duration yard, even tiny metropolis plots. If your beds are tons much less than 4 toes massive, you may no longer need to walk inside the dust inner (1.2m). This makes digging with a shovel even less crucial as it keeps the ground from getting too difficult. You do not need to use raised beds, however the edges help maintain the extra natural stuff in area.

Weeds slowly die out in a no-until garden due to the fact mulches try to suffocate and weaken them. Also, since you do now not dig, seedlings growing inside the soil below the floor will in no way want to arise to increase.

You do store time at the identical time as you use no-till. I can't trust human beings are despite the fact that digging! If we do no longer recognize approximately the soil, it's higher for our backs, the flora we grow, and the treasured soil we use for our plant life.

Growing plants from seeds is a fantastic way to start gardening early within the yr. It's easy to expand a few element from a seed to a harvest with the proper lighting fixtures and some easy device. At first, it's far outstanding only to increase a small quantity of cultivars due to the fact beginning seeds for each plant are one-of-a-type.

Marigold seeds and tomato seeds are each easy to begin indoors. Basil, zinnia, coleus, nasturtium, and cosmos are proper for beginners. If you're a newbie, begin with the ones seeds and then flow into on to more tough ones, like peony seeds. Here are seven belongings you need to do earlier than you may start planting seeds.

Step 1: Time matters proper.

Starting seeds indoors prepares them to head out of doors at the same time as the weather is proper. The seed package have to say while to plant the seeds, so appearance there first. Most of the time, it says, "Grow interior 6–8 weeks earlier than wintry weather." You need to start beans and squash outside. Since they broaden speedy, there may be no motive to preserve them indoors. It is higher to develop a few plants outside, like poppies. Most of the time, those seeds are marked "proper now sow."

Step 2: Choose the proper boxes.

You can plant seeds in almost any box as long as they'll be to a few inches deep and function holes for drainage. Growing seedlings in yogurt boxes, milk cartons, or paper cups is probably thrilling for those who love to do topics themselves. I like how clean it is to start seeds in trays made for this reason. The trays are clean to fill, and the way they water maintains the water diploma everyday. They also are easy to transport.

Step 3: Prepare the soil for planting.

Choose seedling-made potting soil in your flowers. Use new potting soil for your own home flora rather than lawn dirt. Start with a logo-new, disease-unfastened mixture to make certain the seeds are healthful and disorder-free. Wet the planting combination in a bucket or pail earlier than putting it inside the pots.

It need to be crumbly with out being sticky, and it should be moist with out being soggy. Fill the pots to the pinnacle with soil and p.C. Them down, so there aren't any gaps. Because maximum combos don't have lots or any nutrients, you want to feed the seeds nutrient solution some days after they hatch and hold doing so until you plant them inside the soil.

Step 4: Begin planting.

Find out how low to plant your seedlings with the aid of the use of using studying the seed bundle deal. Smaller ones may be positioned right on the soil's ground. Larger seeds want to be buried. As a precaution, I placed seeds in every cellular (or pot). If every seeds grow, I'll lessen one off and preserve the alternative developing. Make some holes in each pot to help the seeds expand. After you have located a seed in every hole, you could cover the seeds. Use a sprayer or a small irrigation bucket to water the ultra-modern seedlings. Cover the boxes with Saran wrap or a dome-fashioned piece of plastic that drapes over the plate to assist the seeds develop quicker. This allows the seeds expand with the aid of the usage of keeping them moist. Take off the duvet as quick as the first green leaves seem.

Step five: Water, feed, and do it all yet again.

A sprayer or a small watering can hold the soil wet but now not soaked whilst the seedlings extend. Let the soil slowly dry out when you water it. Install a fan to maintain the air shifting and live healthy. The timer that runs me increase lighting fixtures moreover runs the fan I use. Mix liquid fertilizer in step with the package deal's commands and regularly positioned it at the sprouts.

Step 6: Continue to reveal to the sun.

For seedlings to amplify, they need mild. Choose a south-coping with window in case you need to broaden flowers there. Turn the pots regularly, so the plants do no longer start to lean towards the moderate. Seedlings will enlarge tall and inclined inside the occasion that they do not get enough mild. If you're growing your vegetation with lighting, make sure the seed heads are just a few centimeters above the lighting fixtures. Use a fifteen-hour timer to expose the lighting fixtures on each day. Remember that seedlings moreover want color to rest. You have to reveal on greater lights because the seedlings increase.

Chapter 7: Storing And Selecting Seed

People have stored seeds for as long as they have got grown gardens. Growers used to think that the seeds from their first-class flora have been provides which have been generally in reality sincerely well worth some element. There are new species to strive every year, and seeds and plant life are cheaper. Here are the maximum important processes to hold seeds alive.

Why saving seeds is critical

The foremost purpose to hold seeds is so that you can preserve growing your preferred plants. It may be the incredible pumpkin, tomato, or blue campanula that tastes precise. We do no longer recognize on the identical time as your favored form of seeds can be taken off the marketplace to make room for modern ones. Only in case you keep your seed are you able to be sure.

What Seeds Can Be Saved?

Only plants that may be pollinated with the resource of some thing or self-pollinating heirlooms will expand actual from seed. This method that the toddler plant life will look much like the determine plants. You might want to keep those seeds.

Different flora will develop from hybridization seeds with both determine or both traits. Most, if now not all, of the flowers you can purchase these days, are crosses. A seed enterprise enterprise may additionally need to make a plant with the traits they need with the resource of crossing absolutely one in all a kind sorts of plants. This permits them preserve their jobs. You can not even shop seeds from hybrids in case you do not want to investigate a few component new. But with the aid of manner of taking cuttings from your chosen plants, you could broaden more of them.

Also, plants pollinated thru bugs or the wind can also have mixed with flora of a different species and won't growth right. All in all, seeds can be used to develop many terrific plants, and the number one "seed savers" have been people who saved and traded seeds. Beans, artichokes, fennel, lettuce, peppers, and beans are some of the proper plants to preserve alive. Some data flora, like cleome, foxglove, crepe myrtle, nasturtium, peony, and zinnia, have seeds that you may preserve.

How to Keep Seeds That Have Been Cross-Pollinated

To get seeds from plants that move-pollinate with contributors of their species, you want to cut up the terrific species physical. The vital strategies to do that are as follows:

1.   Only one type of a species is grown: To try this, you want to put the unique varieties of seeds in wonderful places as you plant them. Different species need to be in outstanding places, a number of which may be very a protracted way away. Pumpkin vegetation will want a half of of-mile, but peppers may only need 500 toes.

2.   Different plants on splendid plants: One manner to do this is to region up a bodily barrier, like a sack or a row cowl. To make certain that each variety receives enough day ride in the open to be pollinated by way of using one in every of a kind plant life of the equal kind, you could have to wrap one type at a time.

How to store seeds and while to do it

Choose the excellent seeds when saving them from flowers, flowers, fruits, and vegetables. Look for robust, tasty, proof against pests, and effective plants. Only the seeds we plant this year will decide how well plants increase next twelve months. When is it best to build up seeds?

1.   When the seedlings of a plant like broccoli, beans, or lettuce die, the pods will flip brown. Some pods will open on their very personal and start to broaden. You can get the seeds thru lowering off the flowers actually earlier than they are absolutely dry and setting them upside down in a brown paper bag. When the seed cones look like they may be about to burst, you could additionally placed small luggage over them.

2.   When the fruit or vegetable (like squash, tomatoes, eggplant, and peppers) is ripe: So, while the seeds are ripe, the veggies might be well beyond the factor of being healthy to be eaten. Most vegetable seeds may be taken out and dried with a spoon. Tomatoes need water to be worked on.

How to Save Seeds and Keep Them

Before placing the seeds away, they want to be truely dry, or they may flow lousy or increase mold. Get rid of as a bargain trash as viable. Keep in a cardboard envelope the choice of the species and the one year written on it. Put the paper in a canning jar or some distinctive hermetic subject. Keep in a place that is bloodless, dark, and dry. The exquisite element to do is store seeds for the following three hundred and sixty 5 days. You can get hundreds of help if you want to save seeds as a hobby—human beings and companies from all around the international list and change their stored seeds.

Plants grown from seeds you stored from your backyard receives used to it in a unique way through the years. Think approximately how a seed is the simplest vintage detail whose fee will increase over time.

Common Gardening Mistakes to Avoid (Section C: Post Planting)

Even in spite of the reality that there is a lot to discover about gardening, it's far a fun hobby that is properly certainly genuinely worth the time and effort. Follow this advice from seasoned gardeners to avoid and join a number of the maximum not unusual gardening mistakes.

Mistake 1: Starting Big

Setting up a too-huge garden is a mistake that could make a gardener unhappy and tired.

The fantastic manner to garden the primary one year is to begin small and handiest plant some of your chosen plant life.

This will help your lawn higher and make you experience like you've got were given completed extra. As you research extra about gardening and get higher at it, you can make your garden large with each planting season.

Mistake 2: Improper Soil Preparation

No garden can develop without healthy soil. Before flowers can increase, the soil want to be organized in some element way is needed. Once the seeds have began out to broaden, the soil can't be changed without hurting the younger, fragile vegetation.

Set the floor as close to as viable to the starting point with out making dirt pies. Wait till the climate is heat enough for seeds to sprout and more youthful vegetation to develop earlier than you loosen the soil.

Then you may start planting the lawn and watch it develop.

Mistake three: growing a desire not to smoke

Vegetables want moderate to expand properly and ruin down minerals within the soil and water. Make nice the flowers you want to make bigger inside the spot you select out to your lawn gets enough sun there. When planning your lawn, you need to hold in mind that a few plant life want greater sun than others.

Read the planting instructions for each shape of seed in advance than identifying wherein to plant it. Some vegetation want to be in the solar all day, on the same time as others do higher inside the coloration. There might be commands on the seed packs. Make a plan in your vegetable garden earlier than you start making different plans. Put the flowers that need the maximum solar in which they'll get full solar.

Mistake four: Inadequate Fertilizing

Your lawn vegetation may not develop properly and sturdy in case you fertilize them an excessive amount of, too little, wrongly, or at the incorrect time. For instance, all plant life want nitrogen, and fertilizer immoderate in nutrients will make the tops increase quickly, that's right for leafy greens like spinach, lettuce, and broccoli.

But the identical quantity of nitrogen will make the top boom so strong that it is able to make the plant take longer to gather maturity.

The equal detail might also need to seem if too much nitrogen on inexperienced vegetables. Don't be too tough with the compost and home made manure used to expand your tubers.

If too much manure or compost is used on a potato crop, each correct nitrogen resources, the top boom can be bizarre, and the tubers can also take longer to form.

Mistake five: Not Enough Watering

Plants want water to develop and damage down meals, but outstanding styles of veggies want first rate quantities of water. Plants will die rapid in the event that they do now not get enough water. Keep your vegetable seedlings from wilting too much for the reason that maximum plant life may not get higher even in case you water them. Only wholesome roots can get nitrogen from the air and hold the plant without delay. The roots can be harm by using the use of using too much water.

The plant will die as speedy due to the fact the roots start to rot. Most plants want to be watered as quickly as to a few times each week with a deep soaking.

If you water too near the floor, the roots may not go downhill to find out water. They will rather expand near the ground.

Chapter 8: Ways To Carry Out Soil Maintenance

Is your lawn sparse and unkempt? Doesn't loads increase on the landscaping flowers you use? Are your flower beds uninteresting? Not getting loads out of your crop? Your soil is probably the problem, and giving it the proper care is the important thing to getting your plant life to bloom, live healthy, and make extra food. You only want to take a few smooth steps to enhance your soil, which is ideal information. Here are a few subjects you could do to preserve your soil healthy.

Test the Soil

Before in search of to beautify your soil, you need to recognise wherein it's miles now. A quick take a look at at a network extension workplace (see Chapter 3), garden maintain, or landscaping enterprise can will let you recognise what form of soil you've got got were given, how tons natural be counted it might have, what its everyday pH degree is, and the way properly it holds water. Once you understand how your soil ranks, you may art work to improve it or repair any problems you find out.

Too many stones are taken out.

Stoney soil is probably the hardest to art work with as it's tough to drill into, it's miles difficult for plants to area down roots, and it's miles difficult to tell in which the water is going. If you need to make the biggest changes, like a new garden format or flowerbed, you may use a rock shovel or a soil nice mesh strainer to take away the worst rocks in your soil. Only a few centimeters of rocks want to be taken out of the topsoil to make a big distinction inside the first-class of the soil.

Think about giving the dirty air.

When the soil can be very hard or has quite a few clay, it is hard for flowers to increase strong roots and now not hold water thoroughly. After the soil is aerated, it will fast absorb water and permit in more air. While you do that, you want to sift the ground plugs, so that they do no longer block the air holes. This will assist loosen up all of your soil.

Add in herbal compounds.

Adding more herbal rely to the soil can assist with many stuff and provide you with everything you need to growth more meals. You can upload chopped leaves or compost to the top few inches of soil or cowl the soil with old herbal manure and allow it damage down over the autumn and wintry weather.

The biological depend may additionally take some summers to undergo this way, however the results can be extraordinary.

Change the soil's pH.

Some plants might not be able to expand in soil this is too acidic or too alkaline. If you do a primary soil assessment or a pH test to determine your topsoil's pH stage, you could try to alternate it to help your vegetation broaden better. Acidity will growth even as you upload greater herbal depend but decreases at the equal time as you upload lime or timber ashes. Think about what your vegetation want earlier than changing your soil's acidity.

Add Beneficial Insects

Even if you do not like how a few bugs, bugs, and caterpillars act in your garden or outdoor, they're very critical for wholesome soil. They maintain the soil nicely-aerated, help flip organic depend into minerals that plants can use, and their waste offers greater nutrients to the soil. You can increase extra worms in your backyard and flower gardens in case you want to. If you can, strive not to apply pesticides simply so useful insects can live in a strong area.

Put down the right type of fertilizer.

The minerals on your soil will be used up fast in case your lawn is growing and doing well. Careful fertilizer can supply those minerals back and keep your soil fertile and entire of life. The superb way to feed your yard, garden, and soil is with natural such things as compost and manure. But you could additionally select from numerous fertilizers made with the useful resource of professionals to install your lawn. To make certain you do no longer use an excessive amount of, which could harm your soil, pick out a product that suits the needs of your soil and thoroughly observe the pointers for the manner to use it.

Remain, Patient,

Preparing soil for sure makes use of takes time, and if the topsoil is in awful shape, it could take years to come to be the wealthy, nutrient-wealthy soil you need. But if you deal with it lightly, it will get higher every summer, and ultimately, you could have tremendous soil that high-quality goals a piece little bit of care each year to feed all of your vegetation.

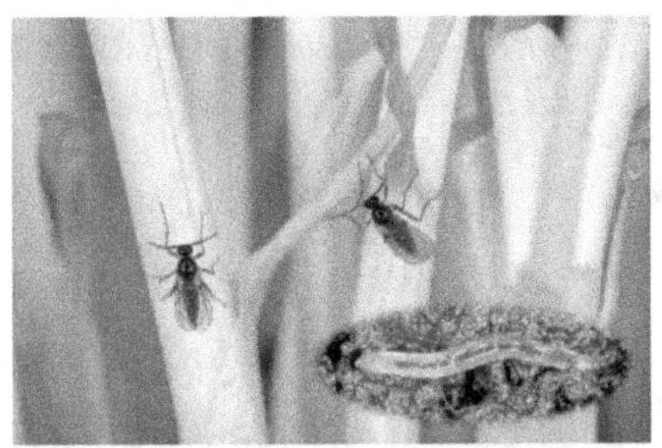

How to Avoid Soil Pest and Disease

Pest bugs and plant illnesses are matters that every one gardeners need to deal with, and they all need to remove them. We count on you have to not acquire for your chemical marketers. They need to rapid save you the attackers, however they might also kill beneficial microorganisms.

You need to throw off the natural stability of your lawn's surroundings and be exposed to dangerous chemical substances through the years. Even so, a natural technique works higher and is extra secure. Here are seven techniques to maintain pests and illnesses from getting into the soil.

1.   Grow your flowers in rich soil: Every 365 days, upload plant rely to your outdoor to make it higher, extra nutritious, and higher able to keep water. Ensure your plants get enough water and food, and add natural fertilizers if critical. Don't make the flora compete for small amounts of nutrients. Use plastic or panorama cloth as mulch to preserve weeds down, and make it a addiction to tug out a few weeds on every occasion you go to the garden. Read the seed packets to discover ways to prune. Spread out your seedlings in order that they

do no longer touch, and enough room for air to flow among them.

2.   Every yr, you may possibly want to easy your lawn: Leaving antique pumpkin vines, tomato seedlings, and a few different waste in your lawn after harvesting is like placing out a welcome mat for insects and viruses. Many insects spend the wintry weather on this trash, and on the same time as spring comes, they start consuming your plant life proper away. Plant sicknesses are always within the soil.

3.   Dead or sick flora have to be pulled out and thrown away: The rest of the trash can be composted or buried. Loosen the soil with a fork or spade just so birds can devour any eggs, caterpillars, or pupae which are though there, or the bloodless climate can kill them. Weeds in your outdoor should be lessen down or removed due to the fact they also can be home to bugs which are a trouble.

4.   Consider crop rotation: Many bugs and disorder-inflicting organisms spend the wintry weather within the soil close to the plant life they live on. If you expand the same plant inside the identical spot the following year, you deliver the ones bugs a huge head start. Crop rotation can lessen the damage finished by means of pests and the threat of having unwell from pathogens that unfold via the soil. You may additionally want to attend years in advance than planting the same crop, like this cauliflower, in the equal spot all another time. When grown inside the identical spot 12 months after 12 months, cruciferous greens, potatoes, peppers, and scallions are much more likely to get ailments.

five.   Promote Diversity: If you located your plant life in smaller corporations in preference to, say, placing all of your tubers in a unmarried spot, it's far going to be extra tough for pests to acquire within the entire task. Another nicely way to protect your garden is to plant spices and wildflowers collectively. Two flowers that don't appear to attract bugs are chrysanthemums and nasturtiums. Others, like dill, mint, and anise, supply in actual bugs that consume terrible bugs on vegetation. Adding some species for your food garden will make your environment extra healthful and additional various.

6.   Plan out your planting: Since insects typically come out at the identical time each year, you could attempt to plant your vegetation so they may be now not growing while the insects are. Keep up with what's taking region to decide out how those dispositions have an impact in your vicinity.

7.   Grow resistant types: Some flowers or cultivars are actually immune to organisms and bugs that reason ailment. Plant breeders additionally try to make vegetation that don't get unwell or get eaten with the aid of bugs. Most labels and seed packets for plants have a list of those

characteristics. Don't positioned too many flora in a single spot, either. Damp locations are proper houses for fungi and specific organisms that can make humans unwell. Things do no longer get too wet when there may be sufficient airflow.

Chapter 9: Season Extension Techniques

A not unusual way to broaden flowers is to

use techniques and substances that make the environment warmer or cooler. This we need to the growing season very last longer. Because of their benefits, hoop homes, low arches, row coverings, and mulch are frequently applied in marketplace gardens and farms.

With those equipment and techniques, you can growth and spread out the harvesting of most gadgets, cause them to appearance and flavor higher, defend them from pests and illnesses, and get extra out of them. They additionally can be used to obtain inside the spring and fall, in advance and later. They may be used to growth flora in all four seasons and to maintain growing inside the path of the shoulder seasons.

No depend in which you live, you can use one or extra strategies on this economic wreck to growth the growth cycle and get the maximum out of your lawn in some unspecified time in the future of a incredible growing season. Most of those recommendations are actual for gardeners of all sizes, whether or not or no longer their gardens are large or small.

1.   Choose the proper one Every vegetable, fruit, and flower is to be had in loads of specific styles and sizes. Some of these will start to develop in advance in the spring or final later into the autumn than others because of the reality they could cope with bloodless better than others. Also, a few cultivars develop faster than others, which shortens the time amongst planting and harvesting.

2.   Choosing the proper spot for your lawn — Some people who want to garden do now not understand wherein to vicinity their gardens. Still, you need to live faraway from the low ground if you could. Because cold air sinks, there may be a large distinction in temperature a few of the pinnacle of a hill (even a small one) and the lowland close by.

three. Use cold frames loads — Chilly frameworks are small containers with glass on top. The glass continues the sun's warmth in the field. Even a smooth cold form may be used to growth the growing season thru a few weeks at the start or surrender of the gardening season. You may want to use any antique window that suits on top of a wooden body as a chilly frame. Don't worry approximately how they appearance.

4.   Use mulch manufactured from plastic – This is a layer of polymer this is going on top of the soil and is pushed down

at its edges. Plants that need hotter temperatures to broaden gain significantly from the plastic that warms the soil under them.

five.   Cover the rows — Crops are stored in vicinity round the edges of inflatable row covers with the resource of placing dirt, rocks, or numerous things on top of them. They can be crafted from plastic or, more often, tough materials that appear to be fabric. Floating row covers artwork like little greenhouses because of the fact they preserve the air moist and pests out simultaneously. Most of the time, you do no longer want to located something some of the crop and the row cover because of the fact row covers are mild enough to flow over the plants.

Methods of Preserving the Harvest

When your lawn offers you masses of meals, you must located it away so that you can consume locally grown meals all one year because it could no longer be prolonged earlier than this smooth, tasty food stops being glowing. So, I've offer you with a listing of six strategies you may store your homegrown meals so you can consume it in advance than it's miles going horrible.

Proper Storage

Many lawn-glowing meals can be saved for a long term and do not even need to be treated if the proper conditions are met. Butternut squash, pears, broccoli, cauliflower, onions, potatoes, and other greens can final everywhere from one to six months, counting on when they were picked.

But it's important to recognize the manner to area topics away: Some fruits and greens very last longer in cool, dry places, like a garage, even as others do nice in cool, damp places, similar to the foundation cellar examined above. All people require protection inside the path of gnawing rodents. Choose healthy vegetables and cease end result freed from flaws, scratches, and scars whilst determining what to store. Some subjects are higher for storing than others. No rotten fruit is authorized!

Refrigerate

The fridge is a splendid modern-day technology that may maintain meals solid for weeks. Fruits and well frozen vegetables will be predisposed to maintain their shade, taste, and nutrients better than the ones saved in one in all a kind strategies.

But do no longer actually put those beans inside the freezer as speedy as you select out them. Before veggies can move within the fridge, they ought to go through a brief method known as blanching, which entails placing them in a warm water bath. This kills germs and prevents the enzymes that change the flavor from running. Fruit may be washed, worn-out, and packed for freezing or blanched and packed in sugar syrup. Raw vegetables like salad leaves, pickles, cabbage, and cantaloupes that have a whole lot of water have to not be frozen. You will likely have a sticky mess to your arms after thawing.

Freezing Jam

If you are new to maintaining, making strawberry freezer jam is a pleasing and smooth start. Most of the time, jams made with this approach taste more energizing, look brighter, and set more impregnable. Making jams on the range takes longer.

You simplest need sugar, vinegar, ripe strawberries, freezer packing containers, and a few fundamental kitchen gear to get began. Each package deal deal of pectin has guidelines for making brilliant types of jams and preserves that may be saved inside the freezer. People looking to lessen decrease again on sugar can use pectin to make jams with little or no sugar. Jams which you make your self can be frozen for up to a year.

Pesto

People frequently consider a exceedingly spiced Italian sauce referred to as "pesto" once they pay attention the phrase "pesto." Pesto is crafted from mint, pine nuts, onion, Parmesan cheese, and olive oil. But even as your backyard has changed proper right into a lush kale wooded location, or you have got a bourbon barrel full of cilantro that dreams for use proper away, it is time to assume out of doors the traditional pesto jar.

Other leafy greens and herbs may be used rather than basil to make pesto. These encompass kale, arugula, chard, coriander, and parsley. With or with out basil, making greater pesto with an excellent mixer, hand blender, or possibly even a pestle and mortar does no longer take extended. You can placed pesto in freezer baggage to feature to soups or greens, or you could placed it in big containers to make quick, flavorful pasta meals. Pesto may be stored for as much as a three hundred and sixty five days without going terrible.

Tip: Use walnuts in place of pine nuts to shop coins.

Putting up meals in a steam tub

When a gardener seems at a cabinet entire of glass canning jars complete of their harvest, it warms their heart. Whether they'll be packed with sweet peaches, bitter applesauce, or excellent baked jellies, they stand for freedom.

But, in evaluation to food inside the freezer, they will be first rate if the strength goes out for a long time. Strawberries and one-of-a-kind excessive-acid plants, like apples and pears, can be well stored at the rack for as a lot as a year if wiped clean nicely and processed in a heat water bath canner.

Salsa

If your backyard is whole of cherries, tomatillos, and jalapenos, you need to make salsa as short as viable. There's no purpose at the manner to learn how to dance. Also, many salsa recipes call for additonal cilantro, tomatoes, and garlic. First, I may additionally want to play upbeat music: When making salsa, you need to reduce or technique many materials, like tomatoes for pink chili, tomatillos for jalapeno sauce, and splendid types of peppers on the recipe and the way rather spiced you want your salsa.

Since peppers vary in how acidic they may be, which lets in preserve food from going horrible, add greater endorsed spices and an acidifying agent like lime juice. After boiling, the mixture is probably colourful and spicy. You can positioned it in containers and put together dinner it for your water tub colander.

Chapter 10: Soil Vs Dirt

How commonly have you ever spent rolling round in the dirt as a infant, and the way normally have you ever attempted to plant a sapling in soil? See the specific phrases that we use in splendid contexts?

I mean, they're basically the same element, right? So why does one have wonderful connotations (of glowing greens, shrubs, and delightful flowers) whilst the opposite has all the horrible connotations (of dust and dirt)?

This question is what we are going to discover in this bankruptcy. First, we're able to have a look at the distinction among soil and dirt, a difference that literally way the distinction amongst life and dying to your flora. Then, we will cowl the basics of soil formation. Lastly, we're capable of find out what regenerative agriculture is, the way it's important to rebuilding soil fitness, and the manner we are able to gain those benefits in our very very personal backyards.

So, with out similarly ado, allow's burrow in!

Soil Is Alive!

The cause soil has such quite a few excessive best connotations to it's far that it's far teeming with life. Not best does soil include severa minerals, vitamins, and herbal depend essential for plant boom, but it is usually numerous microorganisms, which include bacteria, fungi, and unique creepy crawlies. It is a whole environment in itself that supports existence in severa paperwork. Not all soil is the same. Varying portions of nutrients, minerals, and natural rely variety reason soil to have differing residences. As a result, soil in unique factors of the arena consists of one-of-a-type portions of natural depend, silt, sand, and clay.

However, soil anywhere has this in not unusual: it's miles alive.

Dirt Is Dead

Think of soil as a big living organism that drapes the floor of the earth. Now bear in mind rolling around in it and getting it in the course of your garments. That is dust.

In specific phrases, dirt is what takes vicinity whilst we displace soil. Once displaced, soil loses the super matters that makes it a sustainable surroundings, on the facet of nutrients and creepy crawlies. You could possibly as nicely stick a hint tombstone on that mound of muck.

Dirt furthermore motives runoff and soil erosion due to the fact dirt does no longer emerge as compact even as water is introduced to it, because the soil might probably. Instead, it sincerely washes away and takes life with it. Bottom line: you can not develop a lawn inside the dust!

Soil Comes From Dirt

In nature, soil formation is helped alongside the manner thru such factors as climate, panorama, and determine fabric (i.E., rocks, boulders and organisms).

First, boulders harm down into rocks

Second, rocks smash down into gravel

Third, gravel breaks down into the sand

Last, herbal do not forget decomposes and mixes with the sand

The quit end result? Soil! Full of life and ready to manual life in return. Still, it takes time - deliver or take a few thousand years.

You may not command the forces of nature or have loads of years to spare, however no longer to worry! There are severa methods to transform the vain dust to your garden into living soil - all of which we are capable of cover in upcoming chapters.

But first, permit's find out the anatomy of soil and best soil form.

Remember how I recommended you soil is made from sand, silt, and clay? Well, while the ones substances employer collectively they shape soil aggregates. This makes up the shape of soil. Soil aggregation refers to the technique of binding those particles. Why it subjects for your lawn is because of the truth we want soil with a healthy shape chock whole of macro and micro aggregates for it to thrive and be fertile.

A clean, healthful soil form is "granular" or "crumbly", because it includes small clumps of sand and silt held in area with the resource of calcium, clay, and humus.

I recognize what you are questioning, however we're now not speakme about the scrumptious Middle Eastern dip that everybody want to devour with pita bread. Don't fear; I made the identical mistake with the pronunciation too! We're clearly talking approximately "hue-mus," which happens in soil whilst microbes decompose useless flowers and animals. Humus is normally brown or black and is extremely beneficial for the growth of vegetation. It allows in soil aggregation and moreover assets an lousy lot-wanted nutrients for plant growth and improvement.

Calcium, a few other component in healthful soil, is an critical macronutrient that makes plants strong sufficient to fend off pests and diseases.

And subsequently, clay refers to very exquisite soil debris that turn out to be sticky on the equal time as moist and can be molded into severa shapes (think about your adolescence Play-Doh projects). Clay is usually without natural rely wide variety; so, the more clay-like your soil is, the more you will want to amend it for plant boom!

So how do those high-quality compounds suit collectively? Amidst the stableness of calcium, clay, and humus, numerous empty areas shape some of the clumps of sand and silt. In this high-quality association, air and water circulate freely. These areas moreover offer sufficient room for roots to obtain deep into the soil.

Properly primarily based completely soil results in:

Good aeration

Good water retention

Proper drainage of greater water

More essential nutrients and minerals

The improvement of plant root structures

Promotion of first-rate organic hobby (organisms and natural rely)

Quicker warm up time at some stage in the spring

Less erosion

Resistance to compaction

Soil this is an lousy lot greater conceivable

Unfortunately, at the same time as soil lacks the right stability of calcium, clay, and humus, fertility and growth are compromised: picture stunted seedlings and baren branches. If this looks as if your current-day lawn bed, don't despair! Through the miracle of regenerative agriculture, it's feasible to restructure even the worst patch of dull dirt

Saving the Soil via Regenerative Farming

You have probable heard the time period regenerative agriculture, but what exactly does it suggest? Regenerative agriculture isn't always genuinely a unmarried exercise a lot as it's far a hard and fast of practices that sell sustainable farming. Some of these practices encompass the usage of herbal fertilizers, maintaining off chemical insecticides, taking walks with microbes, rearing grass-fed cattle, and using severa crop rotation. Biodiversity is improved, and soil first-class is reinforced at the same time as farmers put in force the ones regenerative practices. These sustainable techniques produce flora which might be particularly resistant to pests and ailments and characteristic a higher nutrient density as properly! In reality, a long term examine carried out via the International Center for Research in Organic Food Systems (ICROFS) showed that soil excellent appreciably stepped forward and turn out to be maintained over the course of 14 years with the use of crop rotation, use of cowl plants, soil cultivation and fertilization.

So, if it is that beneficial, why are not people doing extra of this? Unfortunately, it's taken many years of traditional farming for us to look how actually detrimental traditional practices were to soil fitness. Instead of running with nature, the farming corporation has been treating nature because of the reality the enemy. Think of all those pesticides which is probably closely produced for the destruction of pests throughout farms. They are very truely treating this element of nature due to the truth the satan's private spawn that want to be wiped off the face of Earth. But there's a few different manner! Instead of running at odds with nature (annoying the soil via insecticides, immoderate tilling, and 0 crop rotation), regenerative farming encourages you to paintings with nature.

Regenerative agriculture manner trusting nature's flawlessly designed ecological techniques to take the wheel!This is a healthy method to farming that is more sustainable in the end. And luckily, an increasing number of farmers are waking as a lot as this possibility and making the shift within the direction of regenerative agriculture! And due to the fact a whole lot of those practices can effects translate from big-scale farms on your non-public out of doors, you could additionally bounce at the regenerative bandwagon!

Once you are on that bandwagon, you'll find out that your regenerative adventure involves greater than a shift in agricultural practices; it additionally consists of a shift in attitude.

Taking Responsibility

Did you apprehend that, in advance than and in the route of World War II, 40% of the united states meals produce got here from human beings's outdoor "victory gardens"? That's a large percent! After WW II, that range has been in a well timed fashion declining, and right here we are in recent times!

Let's be actual, on the identical time as we relinquish control of our food to enterprise operations, the primary detail we compromise is super. When the majority of the populace makes a choice to select out-out of outdoor gardening, a large-scale solution desires to be hooked up vicinity. The most inexpensive, fastest, most green way to feed tens of masses of hundreds of human beings isn't going to bring about terrific produce grown with tender loving address the surroundings.

The National Library of Medicine published surprising statistics, citing that over 1 billion pounds of pesticides are used inside the United States on my own each 365 days! And about five.6 billion pounds of insecticides are used global! That equates to form of 3 pounds of insecticides steady with character in the US! Yikes!

The truly horrifying thing is that insecticides come to be even greater targeted over the years (because of a way known as biomagnification) and are chronic for years to come. This technique that we are harming our environment and detrimental our health past repair.

This is why I love regenerative farming. Collaborating with nature in reality affects the first rate of the soil and nutrients ultimately. As I stated, many huge-scale farms are making the pass to this version. However, it does bring about greater luxurious produce. There is constantly a supply and take. So why no longer absolutely implement the ones mind in your small-scale outside operation?

A outside lawn permits you to take responsibility and exchange your manner of lifestyles inside the exceptional viable manner. We can't manage "Big Farma" operations or pesticide use. We can, but, manipulate what occurs in our domestic. We may additionally need to make "victory gardens" the norm another time!

Chapter 11: The Soil Food Web

Now that we understand the distinction amongst soil and dust - allow's begin digging and meet the organisms that make the magic of soil rise up!

As gardeners, we need to transport above (or must I say beneath) and past and have a have a look at everything that encompasses our soil. This approach that we need to apprehend the community of tiny residing organisms that brings soil to existence. In specific terms, we want to recognize some thing known as the Soil Food Web. We may additionally find out how the participants of the Soil Food Web can be beneficial to you in your gardening sports activities!

What Exactly Is The Soil Food Web?

The Soil Food Web is a time period coined through the usage of renowned American microbiologist and soil biology researcher Elaine R. Ingham. It refers back to the interconnections some of the big style of living organisms decided outside and in the soil. Think micro organism, fungi, and bugs. Now combine human beings with flowers, moss, lichens, similarly to large predators like birds and moles all of the way as much as human beings, and also you've were given yourself the start of a cute and regenerative

cycle! You is probably wondering, "isn't that simply the food chain"? Not pretty: the same old food chain is linear, on the same time because the Soil Food Web works from the premise that everything which can consume or be eaten is worried in a cyclical courting.

The Soil Food Web goes to be your nice pal in your gardening adventure. Why? Because those networks of organisms are the number one deliver of nutrients for the flora you develop. Some creatures will form symbiotic relationships even as others devour each different in a selected series after which decompose numerous compounds to deliver all forms of vitamins and minerals within the soil which can be critical for plant boom.

And it doesn't prevent there! The aeration and water go with the flow in soil it truly is vital for existence, is handiest viable thru the movement of organisms thru the soil. This underground bustle of life additionally improves soil structure and reduces water

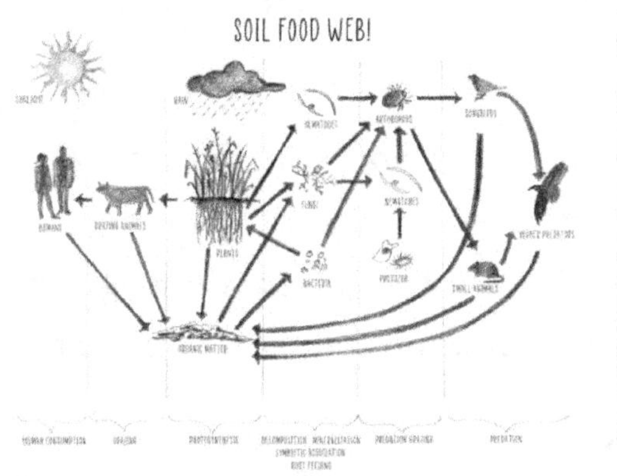

runoff.

Soil organisms additionally assist to govern pollution in severa techniques. This might also additionally sound like a tall order, but the ones tiny soil squaddies are able to changing poisonous substances which include pesticides and heavy metals into benign substances via a way referred to as bioremediation. Some of the larger arthropods furthermore feed on pests on your gardens, permitting your flowers to develop up satisfied and wholesome!

As you may see, the Soil Food Web really is the deliver of all life in this Earth!

Now, allow's take a bit of a deeper study the little microbes you can have as quickly as been grossed out thru and deliver them each different threat via studying them a bit higher. First impressions may be hard, right?

Microbes Give Out Nutrients

I want to consider microbes as glad people on a advent website that get all the material in place for a extremely good constructing. The micro organism, fungi, and protozoa all run spherical diligently with shovels and buckets, arranging the essential nutrients as the foundation for a beautiful form.

Now, our satisfied employees are keen on cycles. In those precise cycles, they take part in a way known as fixation. This is whilst microbes take a specific nutrient and lock it into the soil, developing its bioavailability for the vegetation. For instance, within the carbon cycle, microbes decompose herbal depend within the soil, which releases many carbon compounds that become constant into the soil.

Fun Fact: The greater microbes restore carbon into the soil, the plenty lots much less carbon there may be inside the surroundings.

The equal detail applies to the nitrogen cycle. In truth, a whopping 90% of all nitrogen fixation is due to microbes! Nitrogen-fixing microbes may be decided each in the soil and roots of sure plant life, at the aspect of legumes. Our glad personnel take the nitrogen from the environment and make it bioavailable for plant growth. This is essential in the formation of amino acids and protein. So, subsequent time you've got were given one of these vegan smoothies, you may thank microbes for offering you collectively together with your plant-based totally totally protein repair.

Microbes additionally play an energetic function in some different cycles much like the oxygen cycle, the water cycle, and cycles that include iron, calcium, phosphate, and potassium. All of these cycles and vitamins are vital for plant growth!

Microbes Increase Nutrient Uptake

The amusing doesn't prevent there! Not only do microbes launch nutrients, in addition they make it feasible for vegetation to chugalug those vitamins with out a hassle. The majority of vegetation obtain nutrients from the soil through mycorrhizal relationships, a fancy time period to give an reason for the symbiotic team-usabetween plant roots and soil fungi. The fungi grow in quality hairs and create superhighways that may delivery vitamins, moisture, and carbohydrates like no individual's industrial enterprise! Pretty considerate of them, right? Well, they don't always do it for now not whatever. In exchange, the plant life offer the fungi with amino acids and sugars… just like whilst you bribe your children with sweet! In this manner, both the flowers and fungi encourage each one-of-a-kind, and this all results in a greener, lusher, more healthy lawn!

Microbes Improve Soil Structure

We've all studied in high university biology elegance that microbes help to decompose lifeless plant life and animals. What you couldn't have determined out is that microbes decompose useless microbes too! Microbes can't stay all the time! And even though dwelling microbes feasting on the corpses in their compadres seems like a plot right out of a Tim Burton film, there's a silver lining! Researchers have located that vain and decomposed microbes are one of the maximum strong styles of herbal bear in mind inside the soil, and, as we formerly included, natural undergo in thoughts (humus) is essential for soil structure. Not only that, deceased microbes are the motive that the vitamins from natural depend are retained inside the soil in desire to being stripped away.

It's about time we thanked our glad employees, is not it? I imply, they'll be beneficial to us despite the fact that they are useless!

Microbes Increase Resistance To Disease

Did you recognize microbes prevent illnesses in plants? Plants offer microbes with sugary treats, so in pass returned, microbes fend off the diseases and pests that attack their plant pals to constant their treasured snack stash.

What's extra, like numerous proper friends, microbes assemble plants as a awesome deal as turn out to be more healthy, more potent and greater healthful. They try this via beneficial microbial interest in the soil, which allows the soil produce healthful and illness-resistant flora. We without a doubt owe lots to those tiny creatures.

Now that we recognize the general reasons why microbes are extraordinary allow's shine a spotlight on a number of our microbial buddies: bacteria, fungi, and protozoa!

Bacteria

Usually, while humans say microbes, micro organism are the number one microorganisms that come to mind. Bacteria are the maximum ordinary microbes in the global. Even even though micro organism are tiny, one-celled organisms, a single teaspoon of soil can also incorporate over a billion bacteria! Bacteria are located in specific microenvironments, especially close to the dwelling roots of vegetation, and are particularly focused in the rhizosphere, the slender region surrounding the idea.

Bacteria have taken upon themselves a listing of grimy however essential jobs. They are the number one decomposers of dull don't forget, and they break down pollution and insecticides inside the soil, making the soil biome more healthy ultimately. Some bacteria additionally function as "jail guards." What do I mean? Well, they immobilize vitamins in their cells and prevent them from escaping out of the accumulate in their plant buddies.

Fungi

Now at the same time as someone says fungi, the primary element you can photo are mushrooms: both the traditional crimson ones with white dots from Super

Mario or the scrumptious brown crimini mushrooms you saute with butter for dinner!

But, what you could not have said is that the long-lasting mushroom cap developing above the floor is virtually the fruiting body made thru the fungi going for walks underneath the ground!

The time period fungi in particular refers to the microscopic cells that broaden as long, hair-like threads called hyphae. These strands make their way through the soil, pushing in amongst roots and rocks. Hyphae are extremely skinny, nice numerous thousandths of an inch in dia, to be unique! A single hyphae can stretch everywhere from some cells to over 1/2 of a mile! Hyphae also can bunch up into hundreds referred to as mycelium, from which mushrooms also can sprout, or thick root-like cords referred to as rhizomorphs! So, in truth, you may say that mushrooms are absolutely "the pinnacle of the iceberg" of some element a extraordinary deal more complex this is going on underneath your toes!

Fun Fact: Yeast, a unmarried-mobile organism, is likewise categorized as a form of fungi!

Even despite the fact that fungi are very top notch from bacteria in shape and shape, they carry out very similar skills. Fungi are crucial for nutrient biking, water dynamics, and infection suppression.

Fungi are capable of remodel difficult-to-digest herbal rely amount into paperwork that wonderful organisms can employ. As we talked about earlier, those to be had threads make nutrient uptake a walk inside the park for your plants!

The thready hyphae additionally bind soil particles together, developing a strong mass with the intention to boom soil water keeping ability and water infiltration.

Fungi can also assist control illnesses. For example, there may be a fungi that keeps disorder-inflicting parasites known as nematodes in test. There is also a fungi that feeds on bugs which can harm ground flora. So if you need natural pest manipulate, normally invite the fungi to the party.

Bacteria And Fungi Work Together!

Bacteria and fungi create a powerhouse team almost about producing a healthful growing surroundings for a plant. In this phase, we are capable of take a better take a look at rhizobacteria and mycorrhizal fungi.

You see, plant life have a chunk of a problem even as they'll be left to their very non-public devices. They can most effective rent 4-7% of the soil volume they inhabit. Their roots are also very prone and may die with out troubles.

Enter rhizobacteria! Rhizobacteria act due to the fact the plant's personal bodyguard and form an intelligent safety device around the roots of the flowers simply so pests and illness-causing micro organism can't get in!

But there can be every different hassle.

A rhizobacterial colony can not tour, so that they cannot depart their posts and pass from side to side from the roots to the minerals which can be dispersed at some point of the soil. Unfortunately, the colony will lack the important vitamins essential to preserve them in top frame-protect situation with out these minerals.

This is wherein mycorrhizal fungi come to the rescue! Their micro hyphae threads can reach locations that might be inaccessible to every the plant roots and rhizobacteria, especially the micro-pores within the soil that incorporate the bulk of the soil's nutrients and water. Mycorrhizal fungi convey those crucial nutrients and minerals from deep within the soil lower back to the sentinel bacteria and desk certain plant roots.

And, in change for all of this, the plant roots provide food to the bacteria and fungi within the form of sugary glucose! It's a healthy made in soil heaven.

Protozoa

Protozoa are the ones microbes which can be continuously unnoticed. Think approximately it: every body recollects micro organism and fungi… however say the word protozoa, and all and sundry's face goes easy.

So, what are protozoa?

Well, for smooth knowledge, consider protozoa as an amoeba. Amoeba is sincerely one type of protozoa amongst numerous others, but I won't bore you via manner of list the opposite types. However, I will assist you to know one detail: protozoa are definitely as critical to soil fitness as bacteria and fungi. They are located close to the roots of flora, and their most critical characteristic is... ingesting!

Protozoa ought to positioned the fattest glutton to disgrace! All they do is eat, however they contribute to the soil biome however.

What do the ones protozoa consume so voraciously? They devour bacteria.

This seems like a lousy issue, I recognize, however do not worry. When protozoa feed on bacteria, they surely stimulate the boom of more bacteria.

This takes vicinity through a way called grazing. Grazing is much like pruning a tree. Trees develop spectacularly while you prune most effective a bit, but their increase is harmed whilst you prune too much. Similarly, whilst protozoa graze, they enhance the growth of useful bacteria in small amounts.

They additionally assist in sickness suppression with the useful resource of the use of both competing with or feeding on pathogenic microbes. There's even a selected organization of protozoa, known as vampire protozoa, or vampyrellids, which feed on sickness-causing fungi that attack the roots of flowers. Mimicking their monster film contrary numbers, the vampyrellids join themselves to the ground of the fungal hyphae, drill flawlessly round holes thru the mobile walls, after which suck the cytoplasm inside the cell. They then flow into onto their subsequent victim. In this manner, they hold a high-quality stability amongst beneficial and threatening microbes!

As an added bonus, whenever protozoa eat bacteria, they launch nitrogen into the soil. This is due to the fact micro organism consist of a whole lot of nitrogen, lots nitrogen that the protozoa can't procedure all of it and need to launch the greater into the soil.

Now, as a bargain as protozoa want to devour, they get eaten too. Protozoa shape a wonderful supply of food for special soil organisms. Who knew a few thing can be so beneficial to us simply thru consuming and being eaten?

Next, we cover our excellent pals of the soil community; arthropods and earthworms! Alongside their tiny, microbial buddies, these large organisms play a groundbreaking role in the Soil Food Web.

Arthropods

Arthropod is the flowery time period microbiologists use to offer an reason for the creepy crawlies we apprehend as insects. Arthropods are technically invertebrates, this means that that that they have an exoskeleton rather than a spine. They can encompass ants, beetles, springtails, sowbugs, spiders, mites, scorpions, centipedes, and millipedes. And besides grossing you out, every time you convey up a rock to your lawn, how exactly are they beneficial? It appears; arthropods are top notch at shredding.

Imagine tiny micro organism and fungi looking for to feed on huge lumps of lifeless plant residue and rotting animal depend. It might be a slow and tedious affair, proper? Arthropods assist glide this approach alongside thru breaking apart clumps of herbal rely and with the aid of manner of imparting more get admission to to microbes for decomposition.

Arthropods moreover help micro organism in particular strategies. Remember how Rhizobacteria are caught at their posts at the roots of the plant? This is wherein insects come into the photo. Different arthropods help to preserve all kinds of vitamins to bacteria and all varieties of bacteria to nutrients!

Arthropods moreover stimulate the increase of microbes with the resource of grazing on them. Too plenty grazing may be horrific, but arthropods can considerably growth soil incredible through grazing on soil microorganisms in only the right portions. They also burrow across the soil, that is first-rate for shaping the soil habitat and developing right aeration!

Many arthropods like ladybugs and spiders moreover offer herbal pest control!

Last however no longer least, creepy crawlies are super for soil aggregation. What exactly does this advise? Well, arthropods consume soil again and again again; so, on every occasion the soil passes via its guts, the soil is blended with herbal rely and mucus. This method that the fecal rely of insects (which is largely just densely targeted nutrients) is continuously being deposited in layers. Thus, insects continuously flip over the top layer of the soil, helping plant manufacturing as well as the growth of microbes. That's proper; insects help the soil with their poop!

As you could see, creepy crawlies genuinely do no longer deserve the lousy rap that they presently have! They are real warriors, and your soil is probably fortunate to have them.

Earthworms

Would any economic disaster at the Soil Food Web be whole without the aspect out of earthworms?

Earthworms have commonly been appeared to be beneficial for the soil. But what precisely do they do?

First and maximum vital, they help with soil aggregation to a awesome volume. Just like arthropods, earthworms turn over the pinnacle layer of the soil with their nutrient-wealthy fecal remember. And they invent organic keep in mind deep into the soil.

But earthworms furthermore do a little issue very precise within the soil. Have you located that once they dig into the soil, they depart small holes behind? Well, because it appears, those holes can considerably growth the porosity of the soil. This method increased water drainage and reduced soil erosion!

The holes or burrows which can be left inside the lower lower back of are also first rate for the roots of the plant. They make it smooth for the roots to expand and attain deeper into the soil.

Increasing soil aggregation and porosity moreover has one of a kind benefits for the soil. It will boom the soil's water-conserving ability, which means that that there can be extra water on your vegetation to drink!

But the blessings of earthworms do now not prevent there. Just like arthropods, earthworms paintings as shredders too. They help to shred natural depend amount into forms which is probably smooth to devour by using the use of bacteria and fungi.

Hopefully, this bankruptcy has shed some light at the first rate and numerous global of the soil microbiome and helped you obtain a more appreciation of The Soil Food Web! Apart from analyzing a few exciting statistics you may have no longer identified earlier than, you need to additionally be organized with some realistic information on how critical it's miles to foster the lifestyles of those tiny soil creatures to your garden in order to have the superb soil feasible! The relaxation of this e-book is dedicated to how precisely you may accomplish this.

The next time you spot a centipede, perhaps simply in all likelihood, you'll tip your sunhat to it... In preference to screaming and smushing it to oblivion with a rock. I'm still running on that.

Chapter 12: To Till Or Not To Till

Almost every farmer has their personal evaluations concerning the until vs. No-until debate. But no matter how thousands they disagree, they all have one element in common. It's constantly an "either-or" affair.

But it is not going to be us. While our remaining intention is to transport to a everlasting no-till garden, we are capable of rent each tilling and no-tilling practices till we advantage the effects we need! This financial disaster will explain the way to take the awesome of each worlds to deliver a garden that could ultimately hold the no-till manner of existence.

When Tilling is Needed

Tilling is usually known as the enemy of regenerative agriculture. But why? The cause is that farmers are typically tilling soil that has common a notable microbiome. This can smash all of the ones lovable microorganism connections we truly discussed in our previous bankruptcy and set the soil's incredible lower returned to rectangular one. This is why those farmers want to till every three hundred and sixty five days inside the first place. Tilling places you in a vicious circle. You constantly have to remodel your soil every 12 months because you are

demanding the structure and natural environment that might in any other case hold your soil.

But what takes place in case you're no longer starting out with wholesome soil, and all you've got is a pathetic patch of dirt? New gardeners may additionally use the adjectives dry, sandy, rocky, or tough to describe their outdoor soil at the same time as they are first starting out. And obviously, those aren't the sort of adjectives that describe a healthy growing surroundings for flowers. In reality, all of these descriptions simplest point to at least one element: that your out of doors isn't suit to grow to be a lawn. This is whilst you could forget about all of these judgemental seems and proudly acquire on your roto-tiller! In this example, tilling permits you convert your outdoor dust into suitable exceptional soil capable of supporting the growth of flora.

For instance, assume your soil is virtually too sandy. In that case, you may use tilling to comprise natural depend number into the floor and make it healthy and nutritious on your flora. Similarly, in case your soil is simply too difficult, i.E., too "compact," then you may use tilling to break up the crust of the ground. This way, water may be capable of enter the internal layers of the soil, and you may be capable of loosen the soil sufficient to plant seeds and saplings.

You can use tilling within the initial tiers of building your home lawn to expose dead dirt into living soil. This can also want to help you brief get your garden up and walking within the first few weeks.

The trick is that even as you have made your soil manageable over again with tilling, you may then upload regenerative practices including cover-cropping, mulching, and composting. In this manner, you allow nature do the relaxation, and you can permit that roto-tiller accumulate some cobwebs in the storage. Otherwise, if you have been to transport the traditional route and keep tilling each year, this can have a few excessive risks!

Constant tilling consequences in greater soil compaction in the end. And this particularly happens because of the truth, as said earlier than, tilling destroys the herbal shape of the soil. Tilling furthermore reduces the moisture-retention of the soil. If you bypass in and disturb the earth and then do now not something to cowl or defend it, the publicity to sunlight and air way a whole lot less moisture.

The result? A hard crust! The very identical hard crust you aimed to be rid of at the same time as you first began out!

And closing however now not least, tilling also can shift dormant weeds from the internal layers of the soil to the ground. This motives... you guessed it! The germination of weeds in your dwelling house lawn.

That is precisely why that is only a quick-time period answer, no longer a long-time period workout. You honestly do not need to experience like you're on a hamster wheel, seeing the great of your soil regress each 365 days.

So recollect, if you are starting with possible soil, then don't worry about tilling! Instead, you can at once start constructing a no-till device to beautify the wonderful of the soil for the long run.

Three Main Principles of No-Till Gardening

Before you begin constructing a no-until tool, you need to hold in thoughts the subsequent 3 requirements of no-till gardening. These principles are going to be your manual on your adventure to regenerative farming.

Cover it Up

A no-till garden seeks to defend the soil from the dangerous forces of air, daylight, and weeds. This is why it is vital to preserve it protected usually. Thankfully, you've got many options at your disposal to acquire this, be it thru cowl-cropping, mulching, or composting. I advise the use of all three! Each practice brings some component uniquely first-class to the lawn, and you may in all likelihood as well bypass huge or flow domestic.

Keep it Alive

The splendor of soil is the reality that it is teeming with life and electricity. It is our assignment as gardeners to shield this life and power always. But how do you do this? By planting plants, of route!

Planting to your soil as a brilliant deal as feasible is the exceptional manner to preserve the soil biome intact because plant life help the soil in numerous strategies. For example, they convert carbon dioxide into food, crucial for bacteria and fungi to continue to exist. What's more, the Rhizobacteria and Mycorrhizal fungi inside the soil die out once they cannot form a symbiotic dating with plant roots! This is why you need to preserve your soil alive and thriving through planting as an awful lot as feasible!

Do NOT Disturb!

It can also want to do you genuine to expect a large "Do NOT disturb" sign hung throughout your domicile garden. Why? Well, the complete issue of no-until gardens is to hold the natural form of the soil intact.

We do now not want to disturb the internal workings of the soil biome.

Suppose you continue to until your lawn, time and again. In that case, the creepy crawlies is probably eliminated from their homes, and vital fungal and bacterial connections is probably damaged apart as nicely. Not to mention that regular digging will displace nutrients and minerals and pull up the roots of your plants. This is why you have to virtually depart your soil by myself.

Those are the three primary requirements of no-till gardening that you want to hold in mind. So now, where do you start? I've laid out the easy steps you may observe to start your no-until lawn for every the ones the use of the floor in their backyards and raised bed gardeners.

8 Simple Steps to Set Up

a No-Till Garden from the Ground Up!

If you want to convert sad soil right into a fertile oasis, it's miles exceptional to imitate Mother Nature after which actually depart her the hell by myself! Here are the stairs you need to comply with to attain this objective.

1. Location, Location, Location...

Decide in which you need to start growing on your own home. It is important that you be aware about what course your developing place will face. Ideally, you need a place with the most solar, so south-going via is the nice way to move. Do now not installation a lawn that faces north; your flowers will plot revenge on you via dying. However, east and west are one-of-a-type options to location more land to specific use.

East-going via gardens do nicely while planting lettuce, arugula, chard, and kale. These leafy vegetables thrive with 3 to four hours of whole sun each morning. Other veggies that do properly within the morning sun discovered via afternoon color are string beans, celery, or maybe carrots!

You can also take advantage of a west-going through garden and broaden greens that enjoy the longer hours of the overdue afternoon sun. For instance, you could plant a patch of radishes, corn, squash, onions, peppers, and potatoes! Root greens, in fashionable, will do nicely on a west-managing patch.

2. Clear Out Your Gardening Area

Now that we've the area discovered out, it is time to make your patch presentable! Remove any rocks and debris, and strip away the grass and weeds as nicely. This is on the identical time as a hand tiller might probable come, well... In available! If you find out too many weeds on your garden, you can moreover kill them via which include a layer of cardboard at the floor. The cardboard acts as an incredible barrier for weeds and kills most of them in a rely of months. However, you need to moist the cardboard in advance than you lay it down, so do not forget to provide it a incredible spray at the side of your hose. Once the weeds are dead, cast off the particles as outstanding you may so that they do now not come returned to dangle-out you, and DO NOT located them for your compost bin!

three. Test Your Soil

This step is regularly disregarded, however I get hold of as real with it to be important. It is so beneficial to realize what soil pH stage you're working with! The consequences will decide the amendments you could want to make just so your garden flourishes! Check out our whole crash course on soil checking out in Part 1, Chapter 4.

4. Start Composting

Now we get to the excellent things. Once you have got observe through my composting phase (Part 2 of this ebook), and feature become a composting savant, gather into that compost container and unfold a pleasing, thick layer to your topsoil, approximately 2-four inches.

However, in case you're keen to start planting however have no compost prepared, you can continuously buy some to start! Don't worry; I won't select so long as you promise to start your non-public pile proper away! If you have got fertile soil initially, do now not mixture it into the soil; absolutely lay it on pinnacle.

If you're dealing with a mediocre dirt patch, destroy it up together together with your tiller and blend the compost properly into the floor. Add a few water if need be to make the floor more achievable. This is also a incredible time to bury your Bokashi compost (Part 2, Chapter 4). Then located a touch more compost and water at the top for true measure.

If your ground is a misplaced reason (i.E., intently compacted and crusty), you may want to carry out some soil surgical treatment. Dig approximately 12" to 18" into the floor with a shovel and mix in as a minimum three" to six" of compost with some water. Once once more, burying Bokashi compost will do wonders right here. After giving everything a splendid churn in conjunction with your tiller, fill up the patch, degree your floor, and tidy it up with a rake. Then upload a second spherical of compost (2-four inches thick) and water on top.

5. Plant Your Plants

Now we're at the interesting 2d even as you get to place your seeds into the ground! You can do this the old college way through manner of digging the holes yourself and spacing out your flora sooner or later or thru the use of a seeder! This tool can be an investment, but a seeder can save you hundreds of time and problem. Once the seeds are in, you in reality cowl them again up!

6. Fertilize

Once your seeds are in the floor, now will be a top notch time to nourish your flowers with an additional enhance of nutrients thru the usage of herbal fertilizer or manure! Head over to Part 3 to test the entirety there is to understand in this example! You can in fact lay your fertilizer on pinnacle of in which you planted your seeds. DO NOT artwork it into the floor.

7. Protect Your Soil

Mulching is a vital step to protect your soil and your flowers as well! Wait until your vegetable seedlings have grown as tons as about three-4 inches excessive or have their 2nd set of leaves. Then carefully positioned down a layer of natural mulch round their stems, about 2 inches thick. This manner, you avoid defensive the seedlings and blockading the sunlight, so that you can nuke their increase! However, we do want to cover the soil from the sun and different factors. For the entirety you need to recognise in deciding on the proper mulch, head over to Chapter five, in Part 1!

eight. Rotate in a Cover Crop

Once you have got skilled your first growing season and feature harvested the fruits of your tough art work, you need to make sure all of that fertility you truely created on your soil gets locked in and improved! So now could be the time to pick a cover crop! This is in fact a placeholder plant to hold your soil alive sooner or later of the off-season. It is also a key technique to banish weeds out of your lawn for authentic! Cover plants are critical in case you are excessive approximately building a real no-until lawn. For the ultimate no-nonsense manual to cowl cropping, leap to 2nd half of of of Chapter five, Part 1.

And there you move! You've built your self a extremely good no-until garden actually from the ground up! But, before we get into safety, I need to ensure I didn't forget approximately my adorable raised bed gardeners!

How to Prepare Soil for Your Raised Garden Beds

Raised mattress gardening is sweeping the united states of the united states. Probably as it gives an entire lot of advantages conventional gardening lacks. For instance, you may create tall, price-effective beds (corrugated steel is a amazing choice).This method you could without trouble deal with your garden without wrecking your over again! They moreover produce better yields via manner of permitting an extended growing season because of the fact that raised beds warm up quicker in the spring and supply better drainage in case your soil is ready properly. This we could your plant roots breathe less complex! You'll additionally need to address fewer weeds, and doing away with any that appear will become a breeze!

Sounds too nicely to be proper? Well, the only downside, particularly with the convenient tall raised beds, is how on this planet do you fill them with out paying an arm and a leg for best soil? Luckily, there is a frugal solution! And as speedy as you have set them up, you could examine the no-till standards you have got virtually positioned and feature your lawn move on vehicle-pilot!

Filling the First Half of Your Bed

You'll need your most outstanding soil in the top part of your raised mattress. Most flowers' root systems do no longer move a whole lot farther than 12 to 18 inches down. So let's say we are handling a 30-inch raised bed, which is quite tall. You ought to escape with filling 50-60% of that with an awful lot a lot less luxurious herbal depend range, to be able to offer first-rate fertility and reduce your soil fees in half of of!

So what natural rely may hold in mind as reasonably-priced but powerful? Well, permit's start with the useful resource of protective what you should no longer use. Avoid rocks just like the plague! They will create an synthetic water table that destroys unique drainage, and maintain in mind, correct drainage changed into a important reason we started out out out raised beds in the first place! Instead, vintage, dry wooden makes a great base layer due to the reality it'll provide fantastic quantity and finally decompose under the soil. Unlike rocks, wooden enables drainage through using retaining moisture and draining the extra! Using timber due to the reality the base of your garden bed is a German approach referred to as Hugelkultur! Apart from being a a laugh phrase to say time and again in a German accent, Hugelkultur is a quite easy however powerful way to installation your raised mattress! And it is a superb manner to recycle vintage timber!

Pro Tip: Since wooden can take years to decompose, it is going to be staying to your raised bed for quite a while. For this motive, it is exquisite to avoid positive tree species together with black walnut (which produces a toxin called juglone) and tough, rot-resistant woods together with black locust, Osage orange, and redwood. In addition, willow or any shape of wood that possesses sprouting ability want to be lifeless earlier than use.

So what are we able to located on pinnacle of the wooden? Anything from grass clippings to leaves, lawn trimmings, unfinished compost, or smooth kitchen scraps can fill within the bottom of your mattress. These substances will spoil down rapid and set the extent for remarkable soil fine. Do you still have extra room to top off to that 60% mark? You can use any displaced dirt out of your out of doors as filler. As I advised for the floor mattress, your raised bed can even advantage considerably through manner of burying any Bokashi compost you have got got brewing (again, in Part 2, Chapter 4). Once you have reached that halfway mark, top it off with grass clippings before which include your the best soil combo. So now that we have essentially created a extremely-modern-day backside, it's time to feature your growing layer in which your plant's roots will shape a domestic.

A very famous raised mattress soil blend is known as Mel's Mix, named after the godfather of gardening himself Mel Bartholomew of Square Foot Gardening reputation. This combination is manufactured from identical components of mixed compost, peat moss, and coarse vermiculite. It can be pricey, however as a minimum you have were given masses masses much less area to fill now! Another component to be aware about using this combination is which you need to be assured your raised mattress is on a ground that drains well, together with the ground to your outside. If your raised mattress happens to be on concrete or every other hard ground, you can want to use a particular aggregate.

One preference that promotes top notch drainage comes from a custom mixture created thru taken into consideration one among my favored gardening YouTubers Kevin Espiritu from Epic Gardening (check out his stuff!) This blend consists of identical elements animal manure, regular compost, computer virus castings, sandy loam (it is a combination of silt and clay), peat moss, wheat straw, rice hulls, and quality screened topsoil (may be nearby or save-provided). You have now created the final developing environment!

Now, all you want to do is preserve your garden for the future years. But how? Don't worry, just like your soil, I've were given you included.

How to Maintain a No-Till Garden one 0 one

Maintaining your No-Till lawn isn't as difficult as you could count on. It genuinely consists of repeating fantastic cycles among your growing season and stale-season to hold the lifestyles-building momentum for your soil going!

Whether you went with a traditional lawn inside the ground or the usage of raised beds, the upkeep method of your soil is based totally totally at the identical 3 mind we mentioned on the begin of this bankruptcy! Cover it Up, Keep it Alive, Do Not Disturb! Or CIUKIADND for quick! Nevermind, it truely is a terrible acronym...

Chapter 13: Testing Your Soil

Now that we established the basics of installing a no-until gadget allow's get into the nitty-gritty information of the gardening practices I referred to in my 8 Simple Steps. Starting with soil sorting out; pH attempting out, to be specific.

Planting a lawn without locating out soil pH is like laying a house foundation without first checking the substances. Sure, you would in all likelihood get lucky, and it appears you had cement, but what if you ended up with sticks or straw as an alternative?

In one-of-a-type phrases, in case your soil sucks, your garden will suck too. And specifically pH plays a big feature in that!

This financial disaster will bypass over the right pH ranges of the soil and the manner you could preserve them thru smooth and a laugh sorting out strategies that you could do inside the consolation of your own home!

What is Soil pH?

The acidity or alkalinity of some thing may be measured on a pH scale. A pH of 7 approach that the substance isn't acidic or alkaline however in reality independent. As we glide below seven on the pH scale, the substance's acidity starts offevolved to increase. Similarly, the alkalinity of the substance begins to boom as we cross above 7 at the pH scale.

Several factors have an impact on the pH of the soil. This includes the soil's determine fabric and the quantity of annual rainfall that the soil gets. As a end result, many soils can variety from particularly acidic (with a pH of approximately three) to especially alkaline (with a pH of about 10). Few vegetation, like blueberry wood, are exceptions to the rule of thumb and actually thrive in acidic conditions. However, maximum of the vegetation we want to domesticate in our garden require a pH of 6.Five - that is most effective slightly acidic.

So what truely happens at the same time as your soil is not on the right pH degree? All types of topics begin to go out of whack! For example, as an opportunity acidic soils hold a large sign bearing the terms, "You Shall Not Pass!" to the beneficial micro organism which may be so vital for plant boom.

Not only this, but essential vitamins, which encompass phosphorus, aren't available to the flora in as a substitute acidic environments. Furthermore, vitamins together with manganese and molybdenum flip poisonous in particularly acidic situations and grow to be killing your flowers. One sign of manganese toxicity is yellowing or brown-speckled leaves.

Unfortunately, the grass ain't greener (actually) at the alternative element of the pH spectrum. Heavy metals present inside the soil, which encompass aluminum, come to be extra bio-available in in particular alkaline degrees, which isn't always right. Aluminum is idea to stunt the growth of roots and deter the flowers' absorption of various nutrients

In fact, a whole host of troubles appearance beforehand to vegetation that have the misfortune of growing in soils with a pH over 7. For instance, nutrients which includes iron aren't to be had in a form that flora can without problem take in. In addition, noticeably alkaline soils also decrease the supply of numerous essential vitamins. Thus, manganese, phosphorus, zinc, and copper are unavailable for plant growth and development. Your greens surely won't be searching too warm.

Slightly Acidic is the Way to Go!

The best pH level of the soil is 6.Five for most vegetation - it really is just acidic sufficient to offer plant life with suitable get admission to to all critical nutrients. Moreover, this pH level is also satisfactory to microorganisms and exceptional soil-living creatures, collectively with earthworms. Our hardworking microbes call for barely acidic conditions and will pass on strike and refuse to recovery nitrogen in one-of-a-kind ranges.

How to Test

Calling all youngsters inside the house (or for those who are despite the fact that children at coronary coronary heart.) It's time for an impromptu technology beauty! Get your self a soil pH sorting out package deal, and get prepared to have a few amusing!

Most soil finding out kits incorporate the

following subjects:

A mixing chamber

Test drugs

A dropper

A colour comparison chart

pH possibilities for severa flowers

Recommendations for the way to amend your soil

Let's get started out!

Step 1: Get Down and Dirty

Go out into your garden and pick out the patch of soil that you need to check. I advise attempting out at the least 3 to 4 patches of your lawn to get a median reading of the pH stage of your soil.

You moreover do not need to scrape soil from the ground. Instead, get deeper - at least three to four inches deep - and select up some soil from there.

Step 2: Add The Soil In The Mixing Chamber

Use a steel spoon to drop the soil which you have accrued into the aggregate chamber.

Do NOT use your palms - you can have an impact on the pH studying if you accomplish that. Make certain simplest to fill the combination chamber with soil till the quantity indicated.

Step 3: Add The Test Capsules

Remove the top of one of the test capsules and upload the substance internal into the combination chamber.

Step four: Drop Some Water

Use a dropper to fill the aggregate chamber with water to the indicated degree. You need to make certain that your water is not acidic or alkaline. Otherwise, your studying may not be correct. Rainwater is normally acidic, while tap water is normally alkaline. Therefore, your fantastic wager might be to get a few distilled water - it's miles truely unbiased in nature and won't mess together with your readings.

Step five: Shake Things Up

Secure your attempting out chamber with the lid, and then supply it a great shake. Now set the check aside and allow the soil to relax once more.

Step 6: Watch the Magic!

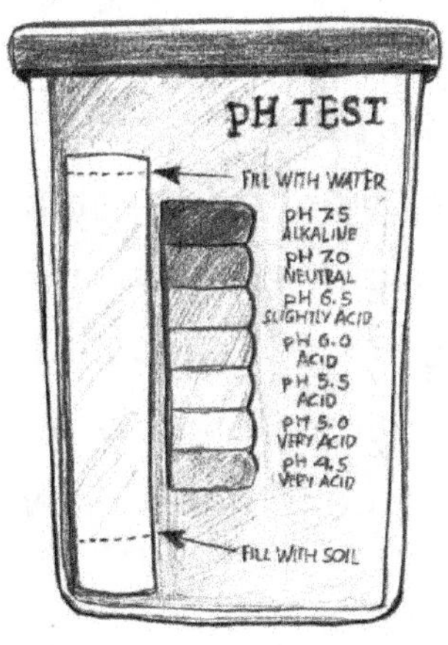

The liquid on your sorting out chamber will trade coloration in a depend of mins. Take the trying out chamber outdoor to look at the color within the daylight. Daylight is desired over artificial moderate so you can get a extra accurate analyzing.

Step 7: Time to Match

Match the coloration of the liquid to the colors at the pH scale. Sometimes, you may not get an unique suit. In that case, clearly pick out the form of colorings that excellent suits the coloration of your liquid.

And that is it! Simple, right? Now, all you want to do is take a look at down the readings from numerous patches of your lawn and take an average of the lot. That's the pH of your soil! So all that's left is figuring out whether or now not you need to make any amendments in your soil or not.

Testing With a pH Meter

Alternatively, you can additionally use a soil meter to check the pH of your soil. The meter is a on hand answer because it does no longer require drugs, paper strips, or batteries. So, how do you take a look at your soil with the soil meter? Here are the steps you want to comply with:

Step 1: Dig In

Remove the layer of mulch you've got were given to your soil. Scrape off the primary inch of the floor of your soil as properly. Use a spade to pick up the soil from beneath. Mix the soil up as lots as possible till you get a homogenous combination.

Step 2: Add Water

Add a few distilled water to the homogeneous mixture of soil.

Step three: Stick It In

All you need to do is certainly stick the prolonged needles of the soil meter into the soil patch. Now, look ahead to a couple of minutes. Takedown the analyzing which you see at the meter. It's no longer as thrilling as a color-converting take a look at kit, however it's miles nonetheless decently correct!

Step four: Repeat

You need to duplicate this way for as many patches spherical your garden as viable. This way, you'll get an accurate analyzing. Then, clearly take the common of all of the readings, and there you pass. That is the pH degree of your soil!

Okay, good enough, so that you do not have a soil attempting out package deal or a soil pH meter at domestic, and also you are not willing to buy one each, I listen you. Don't fear. You can despite the fact that test the pH of your soil. All you need are a few substances you have got were given at domestic. This technique may also moreover furthermore lack the accuracy of the primary , but it still gets the method executed! Plus, it's far continuously a laugh turning normal factors proper right into a technological facts check, right?

Test Soil pH Without a Test Kit

Ingredients required:

Distilled water

Apple cider vinegar or white distilled vinegar

Baking Soda

Soil out of your lawn

Enthusiasm!

Step 1: Get Digging

Gather cups of soil from one in each of a kind regions on your garden. Divide the 2 cups into separate glass jars. Make superb to remove any rocks or creepy crawlies.

Step 2: Get Mixing

First you will be sorting out if your soil is alkaline. Mix half of a cup of apple cider vinegar (or white distilled vinegar) into considered one of your jars of dust.

Step three: Watch Out

Is your soil fizzing? That manner that it's far reacting with the vinegar (this is acidic). In this situation, the fizzing suggests that your soil is primary or alkaline. Is your soil doing in truth nothing? Then which means your soil is acidic, that is why it isn't always reacting with vinegar.

You can confirm this with the useful resource of doing a little different spherical of sorting out. Add a cup of distilled water on your second jar of dirt and mix in 1/2 a cup of baking soda. If your soil starts fizzing, you could finish that your soil is in reality acidic. In others phrases, simple soil will react to vinegar, whilst acidic soil will react to baking soda. This test is a tremendous clean and handy technique of finding out whether or not your soil is acidic or alkaline. Plus, it within reason-priced!

So now that you recognise the pH diploma of your soil, it's time as a manner to repair it. Of direction, if your soil's pH diploma is already 6.Five, then you may honestly depend your lucky stars and begin planting to your garden. But what if the pH degree of your soil is simply too low?

How to Increase pH

There are severa methods in which you may boom the pH of your soil organically. Some of my favored techniques encompass:

Organic Limestone

You can get organic limestone in granular shape and use anywhere from 15 to forty kilos of it steady with one thousand rectangular ft of your soil. Organic limestone consists of calcium it absolutely is high-quality for growing the pH tiers of your soil. I suggest doing this in advance than you do something else on your garden. It is important to get your pH stages up in advance than searching in advance in your vegetation to increase healthily.

Organic Matter

You can use compost or natural rely to increase the pH degree of your soil. For example, 3 kilos regular with 1,000 rectangular feet need to be sufficient to get the pH of your soil the various five to 7 range.

Gypsum Or Lime

You can use gypsum or lime to neutralize a number of the acidity inside the soil and convey up the pH diploma.

Worm Castings

You need to infuse lifestyles into the soil after developing the pH diploma, in an effort to hold the pH diploma at the maximum maximum suitable factor. You can use bug castings to accomplish that. We will discover a way to make your personal laptop virus castings later inside the e book, so be cautious for that!

Natural Fertilizers

Chapter 14: Organic Sulfur

High-wonderful herbal sulfur is soluble in water and is splendid at increasing the acidity of your soil. It is also short to act! You can combo in vegetation of sulfur (a nice yellow powder) into your soil for the same effect.

Note: You DO NOT need to apply aluminum sulfate right here. Many people use aluminum sulfate to change the coloration of their hydrangeas and produce unique fancy effects on their vegetation. However, aluminum sulfate includes hundreds of salt, a substance noted to harm the awesome of the soil.

Peat

Peat is a remarkable way of reducing the pH diploma of your soil. Simply blend it into your soil, and you're nicely to head.

Organic Matter

Organic depend in the shape of compost may be used to decrease the pH degree of your soil. Specifically, compost manufactured from excessive carbonate content cloth, along with leaf mold, has a decrease pH diploma. However, this isn't always as powerful at reducing the pH of your soil as organic sulfur or peat. That being stated, it does make an amazing base in your soil. It also lets in to hold the pH diploma of your soil at an most beneficial factor thru infusing life into it.

Natural Fertilizers

Once another time, you need to ensure that you are using natural fertilizers to preserve the fertility of your soil.

Things To Keep In Mind

There are some property you need to hold in thoughts on the equal time as fixing the pH of your soil.

1. Don't Go Too Fast

You do no longer want to marvel the microorganisms and soil-dwelling fauna with a very unique pH level in a single go. The horrific critters might not be able to manipulate it, and they will come to be death out. Slow and consistent is the way to head!

2. Once is Not Enough

The chemical compounds observed to your soil will slowly carry the pH degree lower lower back to what it before the whole lot become, which means that that you want to hold including amendments often. You can begin with once a month first of all and then space out your amendments in line with your garden's needs.

3. Keep Monitoring the pH Levels

You must display screen the pH stage of your soil after each single trade. And in case you are using malicious program castings to maintain the pH degree of your soil (with none extra amendments), it is probably a excellent idea to show the pH diploma each month or so.

Before we close to, permit's bust a usually believed delusion about solving pH levels of soil!

MYTH: Coffee grinds and pine needles are acidic, and that they assist to decrease the pH degrees of your soil.

FACT: Coffee grinds and pine needles are both too prone or already neutralized in advance than they are able to switch any acidity in your soil.

We have now come to the prevent of our technological know-how beauty. Hopefully, you and the circle of relatives had a few fun with the ones trying out strategies. Regardless, you have got were given taken step one in transforming your soil into a few issue extremely good. Now that you have a chunk soil scientist know-how, you could deliver it a test-up whenever you need to hold it in deliver-form!

So you have got amended your soil, lovingly prepared your lawn mattress and surely planted your seeds. You watch as you become the proud new plant discern of sprouting seedlings. So what now? Do you without a doubt bust out the watering can time-to-time and permit photosynthesis do the rest of the paintings? Not so speedy!

The compost and fertilizer you nourished your flowers with in the beginning can also have blanketed your soil to begin, but that is not sufficient!

That is why this financial ruin is probably that specialize in mulch and cover cropping. We will skip over the fundamentals of every approach and furthermore the way to troubleshoot common issues.

Mulch Ado approximately Something!

If you've got been to go away your beds exposed for the rest of the season, possibilities are you may end up with a difficult, crusty patch, lack-luster vegetation and weeds! Thankfully, there may be a gardening thriller as a manner to prevent this unhappy future altogether. And that secret is mulch!

Mulch is a term that refers to any fabric this is spread or laid over the floor of the soil as a masking. It can come in the form of natural or inorganic material. Not best does it offer an appealing, esthetic contact to your landscaping, mulch additionally guarantees the following advantages:

Moisture retention within the soil

Protection from direct sunlight hours (which prevents the soil from drying out and hardening)

Weed manage

Less soil compaction

Prevention of soil erosion

Insulation from temperature extremes

There are pretty some numerous materials that you may use as mulch, every with their very personal gadgets of benefits and drawbacks. Choosing a soil overlaying can get a bit complex on the same time as you're honestly starting out. But fear now not, I've distilled my mulching guide to offer you the most beneficial and concise facts, so that you can with a bit of appropriate fortune choose out the proper mulch for your lawn.

Top 5 Mulches for your Garden

When it includes mulching your lawn beds, natural fabric is the manner to transport! You get all of the aforementioned advantages PLUS the added bonus that it'll decompose with time. This in addition nourishes your soil. Yes, you can should refill it every season, but your plants will thank you for it! So, in my opinion, it's far great to keep the inorganic alternatives in your walkways and landscaping.

All five of these herbal mulches are super alternatives. But, in the end, it'll come right down to your private lawn esthetic and your budget.

1. Wood Mulch

Whether it is within the form of shredded hardwood, nuggets, or bark, timber is a completely famous mulching alternative. It's debatably the maximum esthetically charming opportunity at the list, as it offers a terrific herbal look even as coming in some of attractive shades! And happily that beautiful appearance will very last loads longer in comparison to one of a kind organic mulches, so it will require a whole lot much less replenishing! Seeing as how it's miles as a substitute cheaper to begin with, this makes it a remarkable bang to your buck.

Wood mulch will also paintings wonders for your garden beds! It has super water retention abilties, brilliant aeration, and pinnacle-notch weed suppression. It furthermore decomposes slowly over again into the soil which include greater vitamins!

Shredded hardwood would be the quickest decomposing desire because it has been broken apart into smaller portions. Because of those smaller portions, it also has a bent to hold water better. Just hold in thoughts that the shredded quantities may also compact over the years, and you might have to break them apart once more.

Wood bark and nuggets will decompose at a slower charge and therefore closing longer. This possibility is remarkable for raised beds in which the soil has a stable border because bark or nuggets will be predisposed to wash away results on the ground after a rainstorm; so preserve that in thoughts.

No depend range range which wood range you pick out out, certainly make sure the dyes are natural, and that your wood is raw and no longer recycled. Recycled timber is dealt with with harmful chemical substances, and some dyes are poisonous! And we definitely need to avoid that! You moreover need to be careful with glowing tree mulch, which has no longer been aged or dried. The easy kind can leach a huge quantity of nitrogen from the soil, so that you ensure you stay with the dried kind to your beds!

2. Pine needles/Pine Straw

A not unusual gardening fantasy you will likely listen is to stay an extended way from pine needles as mulch because of the truth they may be extensively acidic. Though they in reality have a low pH, they in fact cannot decrease the soil pH. Decomposing organisms neutralize the acidity of pine needles as they wreck down and are covered into the soil. As a give up end result, there is no threat within the use of pine needles to mulch vegetable gardens, shrub borders, or flower beds! Even a generous 2 to 3-inch layer of pine mulch will no longer be enough to alter the pH of the soil! Pine needles are a great rate-effective desire given that they'll be free and often simply to be had.

Another variation is known as pine straw, which can be very slight-weight and herbal-searching. Since this option has tremendous interlocking talents, pine straw has a bent to stay installed heavy rains making it a outstanding desire in case your bed takes place to be sloped, or a ground mattress in latest. The one drawback to this mild cloth is that it could not suppress weeds as efficiently as a heavier mulch, so that you may moreover moreover ought to be more diligent on weed responsibility.

Pine needles will correctly keep soil moisture, upload nutrients to the soil, and alter soil temperature. So do now not be aware about the incorrect information and pass over out on this omitted mulch cloth!

three. Grass Clippings

If you are on a finances, then it does no longer get tons freer or less complicated than grass clippings! They also are lightweight and a nutritious supply of nitrogen on your beds! A incredible manner to get the most out of this mulch is thru on foot your glowing inexperienced clippings into the soil as inexperienced manure on the same time as laying dried brown clippings on pinnacle of the soil. Keep in thoughts that whilst most varieties of natural mulch need to be round 2 to four inches thick, grass clippings want to be laid down in thin layers, closer to 1-2 inches. This is due to the fact thick layers of grass clippings can effortlessly lure mould and exude an unsightly fragrance as they decompose. And despite the reality that mould does contribute to the soil-meals net, you probably do now not want to get grossed out thru your garden beds. If this does appear, in truth toss the moldy grass into the compost bin and begin with a easy layer!

Once another time, due to the reality that this material is slight-weight and breaks down speedy, weeds may moreover sneak again in, and you'll want to replenish it often.

four. Shredded Leaves

Shredded leaves are but some distinctive incredible free choice! They include crucial vitamins which includes potassium, carbon, and phosphorus, which may be extraordinary in your soil in the long run. Shredded leaves additionally make clay soil greater fertile and entice earthworms and creepy crawlies for your lawn. Note that the word "shredded" is critical right right here. You have to in no manner lay down whole leaves collectively to your lawn beds. This is because of the truth whole leaves bind collectively and make a robust mat, making it more hard for water and sunlight hours to get on your flora. This is why you have to shred your leaves multiple instances with the assist of your lawnmower in advance than the use of them as mulch.

5. Straw

Straw (NOT hay!) is straightforward, mild, and breaks down with out problem, giving your vegetation more of what they need to increase. The key proper right here is to ensure you select the right straw! We need to avoid hay or straw that may have hay jumbled collectively, which also can motive weed seeds to sprout for your beds. Do your terrific to find out a provider that guarantees weed-free straw. One range is rice straw, which now not frequently consists of weed seeds, however it is not as not unusual as wheat straw. One gain is the volume you could get with a bale of straw. It may marvel you the way lots one bale will cowl when you consider that they arrive very compressed, making it a charge-powerful desire. So start with one, and notice how far that receives you!

Place the straw in a four-inch layer in amongst your plants. However, one word of warning whilst using straw mulch is to keep the straw far from the leaves and stems of the flowers as plenty as feasible, thinking about that there may be a hazard fungus might likely spread on your garden vegetation.

Straw may even decompose specially fast, so it's best to test your layers after approximately six weeks. Making fantastic your layers are quality and thick will help considerably with weed manipulate and maintaining moisture in the soil inside the direction of the brand new summer time months.

Straw is likewise a incredible opportunity on the identical time as planting potatoes! A common exercise gardeners use for potato patches, is they hoe the soil across the plant and pull free soil proper right into a hill around the potato plant. The motive is, that extra potato tubers is probably able to extend along the stem underground. However, in case you pile straw round potatoes in place of developing a hill with the soil, the tubers will expand cleaner and be a whole lot much less complex to find come harvest. You ought to even bypass to date as avoiding soil altogether and in reality using a straw pile which you usually refill!

Pro Tip: Ensure that you are not the usage of any leaves that have been inflamed with spots, scabs, or Anthracnoses (a fungal disease that causes dark lesions on leaves). Also, by no means use leaves, grass clippings, or straw that have been handled with chemical insecticides or herbicides! This will damage your soil and flora! Make fantastic you continuously in my view deliver your mulching cloth.

Honorable factor out: Pea Gravel and Pumice

Even despite the fact that I said in advance that inorganic mulches ought to be relegated on your extraordinary landscaping duties, I idea I can also although include my top inorganic options, if you did want to strive some component a bit greater everlasting. This is due to the reality inorganic mulch consists of materials that do not decompose over the years; the trade-off, of course, isn't any more fertility. Most inorganic substances do now not lock in moisture and will cause warmth stress for your vegetation, the two exceptions, but, are pea gravel and pumice!

Both of these provide remarkable soil protection and weed suppression even as locking in moisture. Pumice, especially, is awesome because of the fact it's far lightweight and porous which lets in remarkable airflow in your soil. It additionally seems really cool!

When is it Too Mulch?

I recognize you are excited to get mulching however do now not get too excited! Over-mulching is clearly a detail, and it is able to result in extra moisture near the roots of the flora (that could cause mold and decay!) and issues with rodent and computer virus infestation. This is why you need to make certain that your mulch layers are usually 2 to four inches thick and not anything more.

The Weeds Came Back!

If done improperly, mulching will now not supply the volume of weed suppression as marketed. This is extra of a commonplace hassle even as the use of natural mulches that smash down fast. So, what do you do at the same time because the weeds hold growing even after mulching?

Spread your mulch early within the season earlier than weed seeds have a danger to germinate

Chapter 15: Mulch & Cover Cropping

Do now not unfold mulch or plant your seeds till you've got got very well removed the weeds from your soil (on occasion hand pulling them is the way to move)

For some component stronger, strive a herbal herbicide with the useful resource of spraying 20% industrial power vinegar on the weeds on a warmth day earlier than planting your lawn (truly be careful no longer to get any in your pores and skin, while you recall that vinegar this robust will purpose damage)

Make certain no weed seeds are sneaking into any of your herbal mulches

Monitor your compost pile to make sure that no weeds are via twist of fate being introduced into the combination

Ensure that your mulch has no longer been removed from its region due to wind or rain

If all else fails, you could attempt together with strips of black and white newspaper underneath your organic mulch cloth for added weed suppression

In end, irrespective of which mulch you pick, usually endure in thoughts to handiest upload it AFTER your seedlings have grown, and deliver your plant life enough respiratory vicinity round their stems. Well that take's care of mulch! Let's waft at once to cover cropping!

What Is Cover Cropping?

Whenever a person asks me this question, I deliver them an analogy of summer season camp. Summer camp prevents children's brains from losing away within the course of summer season damage, proper? Well, that's what cowl cropping does for soil each time it is on its "off-time."

Remember the Keep it Alive rule from the preceding bankruptcy? We realize Mother Nature abhors a vacuum, and if you leave your soil naked for the off-season (or any season), she can be able to gladly fill it with weeds for you. Also, the growth in precipitation within the route of the bloodless season will bring about the erosion of barren topsoil, washing away all of the vitamins! If there aren't any living vegetation stimulating soil-meals net connections to your soil, all of the fertility you labored so tough to build up may be fast undone. Enter cowl crops!

These soil placeholders, regularly utilized by huge-scale farms, additionally translate pretty into the outside scene! The advantages of the use of cowl flora embody:

Suppressing the boom of weeds

Fixing nitrogen in the soil

Attracting beneficial bugs and pollinators into your garden

Adding natural undergo in mind and biomass into the soil

Promoting microbial interest

Improving the soil form and stopping erosion with their robust, fibrous threadlike root structures